The
Miracle
of Easter

Other books in this series

The Miracle of Easter

compiled and edited
by Floyd Thatcher

WORD BOOKS
PUBLISHER
WACO, TEXAS

THE MIRACLE OF EASTER

Scripture quotations marked RSV are from The Revised Standard
Version of the Bible, copyright 1946 (renewed 1973), 1956, and © 1971
by the Division of Christian Education of the National Council of the
Churches of Christ in the U.S.A., and used by permission. Scripture
quotations marked NEB are from The New English Bible, © The
Delegates of The Oxford University Press and The Syndics of
The Cambridge University Press, 1961, 1970; reprinted by permission.
Scripture quotations marked E. V. RIEU are from The Four Gospels
translated by E. V. Rieu, copyright © 1953 by Penguin Press, Ltd.
Scripture quotations marked Phillips are from The New Testament in
Modern English, rev. ed., © J. B. Phillips 1958, 1960, 1972;
reprinted with permission of Macmillan Publishing Co., Inc.

Grateful acknowledgment is made to Frances Brown Price for
permission to use her poem "In His Presence" as an epigraph to
this book; from Blue Flame, © 1967 by Frances Brown Price,
published by The Naylor Company, San Antonio, Texas.
Grateful acknowledgment is also made for the use of chapter 9
from Those Mysterious Priests by Fulton Sheen, copyright © 1974
by Fulton J. Sheen; used by permission of Doubleday & Company, Inc.

Special thanks go to artist O. Stanley Miller
for providing the drawing used on the chapter
title pages in this book.

ISBN 0-8499-2902-4
Library of Congress catalog card number: 79-67613
Printed in the United States of America

For Harriett

My companion and partner in the
pilgrimage of life and in the
quest of faith . . . whose love
and sensitivity have kept me on track
when I was tempted to wander.

Contents

To the Reader

For many years during the forty days preceding Easter I have made it a practice to read through the four Gospels—and read them as if I had never heard the stories before. Each journey through has been a fresh experience of faith as I have endeavored to blank out completely any preconceived notions or interpretations. This quest for truth and understanding has been inspired in part by what I believe to have been the spirit of Kierkegaard when he said, "I do not know the truth except when it becomes part of me." And each year as I have finished my reading during Holy Week, I have moved toward a more intimate understanding of what Dr. E. V. Rieu really meant when he wrote, "The Gospels . . . are the Magna Charta of the human spirit."

In these magnificent and awesome freedom documents we confront an adult Jesus of Nazareth striding to the banks of the Jordan to be baptized, moving on quietly to his lonely experience of testing in the wilderness, and then entering into his intensely active and consuming public ministry. And it was a ministry of involvement on a day-to-day basis with the needs and hurts of people caught up in the ordinary business of trying to carve out a life with meaning and hope.

From those first moments of public involvement a tremendous power was unleashed in our world. It was the power that brought healing to tormented bodies, wholeness to the emotionally disturbed, food for the hungry, and life to the dead —physically and spiritually. And it is the power that has generated the noblest in people of every succeeding century.

It is the purpose of this short book to focus on this same Jesus from the perspective of each writer. These chapters are not for passive reading, for the central figure, I believe, can only be confronted with meaning by the energetic and involved searcher after truth whose mind and heart are not dulled by the familiar or the comfortable.

This is a book to be read at any time of the year, for the awesome events of the death and resurrection of Jesus are not seasonal. But it is especially to be read as a companion to the journey through the Gospels, during those reflective days leading up to Easter. And once again, the miracle of Easter becomes fresh and new because "it becomes part of me."

FLOYD THATCHER

January 1980

In His Presence

As if my reaching heart
had touched his garment,
suddenly, I knew!
No muscle moved, I think;
but all of me
was kneeling
in awe and wonder
in His presence

Frances Brown Price

The Miracle of Easter

Floyd Thatcher

And we went through the whole of
Galilee, entering their synagogues to
proclaim his message and casting out
demons.

(Mark 1:39, E. V. RIEU)

And whenever he came to a village, town,
or farm, they laid down the sick in
public places and begged him only to let
them touch the tassle on his cloak. And
all that touched him were saved.

(Mark 6:56, E. V. RIEU)

"The worst sin towards our fellow creatures is not to hate them . . . but to be indifferent to them; that's the essence of inhumanity."

In this perceptive remark, credited to George Bernard Shaw, journalist, essayist, dramatist, and novelist, I detect a hint of what I believe to be a significant facet of the miracle of Easter.

Sometime, possibly at the first break of light across an indigo sky or at the moment the sun edged above the horizon, our Lord moved out of the tomb on that first Easter morning. And it was at this instant that he brought into vivid focus a whole new perception of human worth and wholeness. Here, emblazoned across the skies of history was the final, irrefutable evidence that Jesus Christ is Lord of death as well as Lord of life.

But for me, the roots of this climactic event are clearly seen months and even years before in the actions and attitudes of Jesus along dusty country roads, in the midst of the bustle of a village marketplace, in the hurly-burly, give-and-take of city life. The miracle of Easter takes on its deepest meaning as I reflect on the actions of Jesus during the earliest days of his public life when he cared enough to heal "a man possessed by an unclean spirit" in the synagogue at Capernaum; when his heart was twisted with compassion and he touched the foul and loathesome skin of the Galilean outcast and healed him of leprosy; and when he was moved to action at the sight of the paralyzed man whose desperate friends tore up the roof in their effort to get him to Jesus. In the country of the Gerasenes it was a maniac living among the tombs who was cured . . . on a crowded

street it was a woman debilitated by a hemorrhage who
experienced healing by a touch . . . in Jairus's home it was
a much loved but dead little girl who breathed new life . . .
in the region of Decapolis a deaf and dumb man was made
to hear and speak . . . in Jericho blind Bartimaeus received
the gift of sight.

To read the Gospel stories about Jesus through
lenses not smeared with familiarity or soiled and spotted by
preconceived prejudice is to confront a Jesus who was
consumed by the physical pain and emotional hurts of
people caught in the agonizing realities of life in a hard,
demanding, and cruel world. There were no signs of apathy
or superficial pietism in his responses. Rather, we see him
outraged by the impact of physical and emotional disease.
He could not ignore tormented minds, crippled and
disease-ridden bodies, or hungry stomachs. He felt the bitter
and crippling pain of loved ones who were diminished by
the death of a daughter, a son, a brother. And even at his own
execution, instigated by the self-righteous religious and civic
leaders whose comfortable ideas were threatened by his
revolutionary appeal to care deeply, Jesus' concern went out
to the mental and emotional suffering of his mother and
friends huddled together watching him die.

The miracle of Easter is in the *impassioned
people-directed life* Jesus lived, and he lived it with a driving,
engrossing gusto. If he had been drab or dull or a bore, I
don't believe the crowds of people would have so engulfed
him that he had to force times of privacy and prayer. A
description of St. Francis given by G. K. Chesterton in his
St. Francis of Assisi could as well be a description of Jesus
and the quality of his life: "St. Francis deliberately did not
see the wood for the trees. It is even more true that he
deliberately did not see the mob for the men. . . . He only
saw the image of God multiplied but never monotonous.
To him a man was always a man and did not disappear in
a dense crowd any more than a desert. He honored all men;

that is, he not only loved but respected them all. . . . There was never a man who looked into those brown burning eyes without being certain that Francis Bernardone was really interested in him . . . in his own inner individual life from the cradle to the grave; that he himself was being valued."

I believe that as Jesus touched and healed and provided bread and wept; as he embraced little children and loved his friends and was sensitive to the feelings of the prostitute; as he ate and laughed with loved ones; he was giving us a dramatic prelude to his earth-shattering death and electrifying resurrection from the grave. And it is through these actions that we come to understand more clearly the startling events that occurred under the power of the Holy Spirit shortly after he left this earth. We see in all of this a working model for making some bit of sense out of life in our highly complex and confusing world.

As I have struggled to participate as best I can in the Easter miracle, the words of John Knox invade the center of my consciousness with penetrating intensity: "The primitive Christian community was not a memorial society with its eyes fastened on a departed master; it was a dynamic community created around a living and present Lord." [1] And for me, the "living and present Lord" is the Jesus who felt deeply—to the point of outraged action—the hurts and injustices of people in Jerusalem or Rome, and who now shares in the suffering of displaced refugees in Southeast Asia, the embattled people of Africa who are struggling valiantly for a niche in the twentieth century, the alienated Christians and Jews in the Soviet Union, and the hungry and sick and lonely in New York or Dallas or Los Angeles.

Jesus wept over Jerusalem, but most of the time my eyes remain dry as my morning paper reports and describes the brutal injustices perpetrated on the poor and alienated, flesh-and-blood people in today's so-called civilized society. And most of the time my eyes are dry as I listen to

---

[1] *Jesus, Lord and Christ* (New York: Harper and Brothers, 1958), p. 118.

the stories of psychologically castrated men caught on the
rack of a cruelly competitive and impersonal business or
professional machine dominated by a bottom line mentality
which robs them of their integrity and threatens their
personhood . . . or as I listen to the agonizing words of a
housewife and mother who is dying by inches emotionally
as she struggles for her own identity and fights a daily battle
against oblivion. At the same time she seeks to be supportive
of a husband ground thin by the system and of children trying
desperately to discover their roles in a computerized and
impersonal world.

But, all too often our tendency is to retreat
from the raw edges of life to what my friend Jard DeVille
refers to as our "comfort zones." There's less risk here and
people aren't threatened. James Pike spoke graphically in a
sermon a few years ago, "Independence of spirit means a
cross. Simple conformity to the prevailing mood . . . spares
one the cross." And so as we practice our sterile conformity,
we become self-contained and myopic within our
inner-circle mentality in an effort to avoid the pain of active
participation.

Halford Luccock in *The Interpreter's Bible*
(vol. 7) describes quite vividly the prevailing mood in so many
circles today: "What would we think of the crew of a
life-saving station who gave all their attention to the station
itself, made the quarters attractive, planted gardens, designed
uniforms, provided music, and thus pleasantly occupied,
shut out the roar of the pounding breakers, driving ships and
men to destruction on the rocks? Yet is such a fancy far
removed from a church, so intent on its own interior life, its
housing, its decoration, its material well-being, that the plight
of those outside, in need of salvation in Christ, is forgotten
or becomes subordinate to other things? The church is not
a company on a summer hotel porch; it is a life-saving crew."
And it is this kind of a model Jesus gave us as he moved

resolutely toward the events of Good Friday and Easter
morning.

A few years before his death I spent several hours
in conversation with one of the most alive and single-minded
Christians I have ever met, Richard Cardinal Cushing of
Boston. Coming to know him just a little through those
hours gave breath and life to these words of his: "It cannot
be enough that the church should merely proclaim her faith
in Christ with the hope that those who hear will turn at once
and confess their faith in him. To engage men of our age
the church cannot begin from the point of authority and
revelation but rather from experience and relationships. The
men of our time are not very much different from those
of the Lord's own day. They must find Christ in others before
they are ready to see him in the Church's teachings."

Resurrection commitment and power cannot be
involved with the ordinary, the superficial, with minutiae.
An unidentified news correspondent in a rare moment of
inspiration wrote these descriptive lines:

> Some men die by shrapnel,
> Some go down in flames.
> But most men perish inch by inch
> Who play at little games.

The miracle of Easter points to a life style not of mediocrity
and littleness but to one of "big games." It involves risk
and venturing and change as we move toward the wholeness
which God has designed for each of us.

Paul Tournier wrote in his *The Meaning of
Persons*, "Life is not a stable state, but a rhythm, an
alternation, a succession of new births." I find that it is
these daily or periodic new births which peel away the
defensive and deadening layers in our lives and expose the
raw edges of our feelings to the healing power of God and

to a sensitive awareness of his presence. It is these moments which take the flatness out of life and ignite the spark of daring to strive for the model Jesus gave us.

I lived just such a rebirth on a recent Saturday morning, after what for me had been a brutal week. Stepping out the front door of our secluded hideaway in the country twenty-five miles north of Waco, I walked under an umbrella of towering cottonwoods the thirty or so steps to the edge of the river. It was about halfway between total darkness and sunrise. The river was running high and strong. And as I looked across the hundred and fifty or so yards to the opposite shore, I became aware of the shimmering vapor hovering low over the surface of the water—a little spooky and haunting in the half-light, but incredibly beautiful. The atmosphere was totally devoid of human sounds—a stillness seldom experienced these days. The only noises came from the rippling of the river as it flowed by and two cardinals perched high in the cottonwoods, who from the cadence in their calls back and forth seemed to share with me the awe and hush and beauty of the moment. Looking up, I saw streaks of red on the few stray wisps of clouds as the sun's rays searched them out in the otherwise unmarked sky. There was a pungent aroma of freshness about the morning air.

Tears formed in the corners of my eyes as I stood there absorbing those moments of the morning, and my thoughts turned to the name given to this historic river by early Mexican explorers and settlers—*El Rio de los Brazos de Dios* . . . the River of the Arms of God. And suddenly it seemed almost as if I was enfolded in the "arms of God," and I felt the assurance that everything was all right. For long moments I stood there taking this in, as it were, through the very pores of my skin.

A distraction on the opposite shore jolted me back to reality. The spell was broken, and as I thought back over the week, a newspaper headline of a day or so before flashed across my mind: "Local Authorities Happy About Execution." In scanning the article I had read where a local federal judge expressed satisfaction over the execution in Florida of the first person to be legally put to death in the United States in two years. And the District Attorney implied that if a few more criminals "fried," incidents of capital crime would diminish.

The gross insensitivity of our quivering world suddenly pressed down hard on the exposed edges of my feelings. For a few brief moments a stifling blanket of depression shut out the emerging radiance of the morning.

But then, the throaty calls of the cardinals pierced my consciousness once again. And almost as if on cue I picked up the tired-sounding hoot of a great white owl who nests in one of our huge pecan trees. The ripples along our shore seemed to whisper the eternal assurances of a God who cares. And once more I saw and felt God in the morning, and once more I was reborn to move out again to confront with boldness the needs and concerns of people wherever we passed each other.

During a later moment in that climactic morning, my thoughts turned back to another period of rebirth which I feel changed the course of my life. She was seventy-eight and I was thirty when we first met years ago. In many ways it was an unlikely relationship, but we were closely associated until her death twelve years later. Through her *Streams in the Desert* Mrs. Charles Cowman was many things to many people. Her roots were deep in Philadelphia society and in old, historic St. Stephen's Episcopal Church where so many of her family were buried. Her pilgrimage and her passion for the spiritual and physical welfare of people had taken her to Japan and China—and from there to more than a score of countries on most every continent. It had made her a confidante and friend of such diverse world leaders as Madame Chiang Kai-shek and Emperor Haile Selassie.

But she was God's instrument to open my
eyes just a little to where I caught a fleeting glimpse of the
wideness of God's mercy. She started me on a pilgrimage of
inclusive faith—one that involves a commitment to feeling
and sharing in the physical pain and emotional hurts and
alienation of the people that move in and across my life
through whatever means. Her deeply lined face and white
hair spoke of the difference in our years, but her daily mood
of eager expectancy and her sensitive passion for the healing
of people exemplified in living color the message and
ministry of Jesus. It was during our hours together that
she gently nudged me out of my self-containment and
satisfaction—out of my comfort zones—into a world of
feeling and caring and action.

But to look back again, the devastating events
of that first Good Friday left the very people who had
walked with Jesus for more than three years absolutely
paralyzed. The blind who saw . . . the deaf who heard . . .
the crippled who walked . . . the dead who breathed again . . .
all of these were forgotten as Jesus' followers groveled
behind closed doors. They hadn't heard him when he said,
". . . we are going up to Jerusalem. The Son of Man will
be handed over to the Chief Priests and the Doctors of the
Law. They will condemn him to death and give him up to
the pagans, who will mock him and spit at him and flog him
and put him to death. And after three days he will live again"
(Mark 10:32–34, E. V. Rieu). The model Jesus gave them
for believing and caring and sharing and helping disappeared
from their minds like a faded mirage. Hope was gone and
crippling despair smothered them.

But the drama and the miracle of that first Easter
dawn—the resurrection of Jesus Christ—revolutionized all
of creation. The immediate impact of the miracle was seen
in the dramatic change in the lives and actions of those
confidants of Jesus who were fearful and had gone into
hiding at his death. Now they had moved out into the open

with seeming reckless abandon in their Spirit-intoxication. Then pathological fear and self-concern were converted into an impassioned caring for the physical, social, and spiritual needs of people. Peter and John clearly epitomize the mood of those moments when they confront the begging lame man at the Beautiful Gate of the Temple. Their answer to his request for money didn't evoke a sermon or a proof text; rather, in response to the beggar's deepest need Peter reached out and touched him in the name of Jesus of Nazareth, and "at once his feet and ankle bones were strengthened, and he sprang to his feet, stood and then walked" (Acts 3:1-8, Phillips). Further proof of change is expressed a little later: "Many signs and wonders were now being shown among the people. . . . People would bring out their sick into the streets and lay them down on beds or stretchers, so that as Peter came by at least his shadow might fall upon some of them. . . . And they were all cured" (Acts 5:15-16, Phillips). And in another place we discover that they cared for each other so much that not a single person in their group had a need unmet.

Leslie Weatherhead in his *Key Next Door* sums up the atmosphere of those days with these words: "Within seven weeks they—the hunted, frightened fugitives—had become flaming missionaries and willing martyrs ready to lay down their lives rather than deny the truth of His risen glory and His transforming power. Christianity was launched on its world mission."

And the drama and the miracle of Easter today is uniquely expressed, I believe, in these words of Frederick Buechner in his *Telling the Truth*: it is "the outlandishness of God who does impossible things with impossible people."

"For if a man is in Christ he becomes a new person altogether—the past is finished and gone, everything has become fresh and new" (2 Cor. 5:17, Phillips).

Despair: A Human No

Harold C. Warlick, Jr.

He was despised and rejected by men;
   a man of sorrows, and acquainted with
      grief;
and as one from whom men hide their
      faces
   he was despised, and we esteemed him
      not.

(Isaiah 53:3, RSV)

"*If you stand on the courthouse steps long enough, the* parade will come back around." This laconic comment by the late Dr. Carlyle Marney, eminent minister, theologian, and philosopher, refers to the tendency for the elements of life to move in a circle and repeat themselves. There is no question that recurrent themes are a part of the very stuff of living.

There's probably no better reflector of this phenomenon than television. Some twenty years ago when I was growing up, Tuesday night television featured "The Millionaire." In this extravaganza, each week an incredibly wealthy man gave a million dollars, tax-free, to an unsuspecting but worthy person, and with this windfall each of these new millionaires was able to put feet to lifelong dreams and fantasies.

Recently, "the parade came back around" in the form of a program called "Fantasy Island" in which the lead character specializes in making people's wildest dreams come true. But there's an intriguing twist to the plot. In every case the fulfillment of the fantasy precipitates a crisis whereby the people come to recognize that bogus promises have deceived them and they either come to grips with some great moral truth or find fulfillment in a new and unexpected way.

One particular "Fantasy Island" episode had special appeal to me and certainly raised my awareness level several notches. It seems that a prince arrived on the island and asked to be allowed to fulfill his fantasy of living like a common man. From his sheltered vantage point in life, he simply couldn't understand the ordinary person's scramble for money and status.

The prince's wish was granted—his identification was removed, his money was taken from him, his fine clothes were exchanged for an old work uniform, and he was given a menial job on the crew of a fishing trawler.

With his new identity the prince began to discover a thousand little human no's which he never knew existed before. One evening he attempted to enter a posh country club to meet a girl but was turned away at the door because he wasn't a member. On another occasion he was refused admission to an elite restaurant because he was improperly dressed and had no coat and tie. When he attempted to date certain girls from the island's high society, they would have nothing to do with him because he was only a poor, and at times smelly, fisherman with no apparent prospects for advancement.

It was a rude awakening for the prince as he attempted to claw his way through an utterly alien world—one he had never known existed . . . the shattering world of the human no which casts a contaminated cloud over human spirits in today's humdrum world.

In a sense, much of our day-to-day routine in one way or another involves confrontation with the world of no and our subtle, and sometimes not so subtle, maneuverings and manipulations to sidestep obstacles and get our way. For example, I have a friend in Boston who understands the mental and psychological makeup of headwaiters. On one occasion I was complaining to him about having to wait an abnormally long time for a table in a fashionable French restaurant. No problem, he responded. "Always check in as Dr. Warlick, not Mr. Warlick or the Warlick party. They always let the doctors in first."

And so it seems that, when we give careful thought to it, we devote an enormous amount of our time and energy to acquire position and resources which will enable us to open the closed doors of human no.

But amazingly enough, the ontological world, the

world of *being,* is also pervaded by the human no. Rejection, sorrow, and death are closed doors which block out our clear view of the future. John Masefield, in a poem entitled "The Widow in the Bye Street," depicts graphically a heart-wrenching scene that illustrates the no's in the world of being. In the poem a young man is executed by hanging for crimes committed against the state. His mother is in the crowd that witnesses the sordid scene. As the young man's body gives up the struggle, the pathetic mother sobs and mumbles, almost to herself, something about "broken things too broke to mend." What anguish and hopelessness saturate those words; here is the essence of depair—a past and a present, but no future.

There is much about life even in our sophisticated late twentieth-century world that seems "too broke to mend." We witness the deaths of loved ones and friends who were "too broke to mend." Marriages collapse that are "too broke to mend." People's dreams are shattered and "too broke to mend." Despair, the threat of nonbeing, is always the product of circumstances which seem "too broke to mend." And yet it is at this very moment in life that the events of Easter shout a word of hope and victory.

From the depths, the prophet Isaiah describes one who is "despised and rejected by men; a man of sorrows, and acquainted with grief; and as one from whom men hide their faces he was despised, and we esteemed him not" (Isa. 53:3, RSV). What an apt description of Jesus as viewed from the world perspective.

Without question, Jesus felt the ugly and loathsome human no. He felt rejection and heard the frenzied roar of his own countrymen clamoring for his execution. He had felt the identifying kiss of a friend who betrayed him to his enemies, had heard the denial of friendship by someone very close to him, and had stood the humiliation of an illegal trial in the middle of the night. Certainly the crushing and stifling weight of the human no

came crashing down on the head of this young man of
thirty-three. Here, indeed, were "broken things too broke
to mend."

But the world of hundreds and possibly
thousands of other people was also shattered by his
ignominious and cruel death. He had appeared as the
looked-for Messiah, and people were stirred and deeply
moved with excitement—for a time it seemed that the shackles
of physical and emotional oppression imposed on them by
Rome would be broken. Freedom of body and spirit was
in sight. And then the arrest, trial, sentence, and death of
Jesus seemed to drop the curtain on all their hopes—the
human no had won out again and a smothering despair
seemed to wipe out all possibilities for the fulfillment of
their dreams.

Dr. E. Stanley Jones, world missionary leader
and author of many books, commented one day that a
friend of his insisted that he just could not accept Christ as
Lord of his life because he couldn't follow a loser. He
believed firmly that anyone who died on a cross and was
defeated by the world's no was a loser.

By contrast, Nels Ferré, in his remarkable little
book entitled *The Extreme Center*, tells about an experience
he had one day in Marburg, Germany. In his search for truth
he had been reading German theology for several weeks, but
found it a dry and empty experience. On one particular day
he decided to visit St. Elizabeth's Church, the historic
cathedral built in honor of the woman credited with the
establishment of Christian hospitals. As Ferré walked into
one of the small chapels, he was confronted by a rather
awesome-looking two-level sarcophagus. On the very top
reclined the figure of a Teutonic knight dressed in the splendid
glory of his most festive battle regalia. Here was man
portrayed at his noblest and best, at the very peak of his
earthly splendor.

But the lower level of the sarcophagus depicted

a jarring contrast. Here was the same knight, but now he was a decaying corpse overrun by snakes and disgusting-looking toads. The two levels of this sarcophagus illustrated the vanity of life: "No matter how high the glory, there's always the same end to the story, decay and rot"—the human yes destroyed by the human no.

Ferré tells how he moved away from that scene with wretched feelings of weariness and depression. And a few minutes later, while walking through the main part of the church, he caught sight of an old crucifix on the wall. That rather crude but highly suggestive symbol of a life broken in concern and love for the world spoke at that moment to his inner needs as nothing else had. Suddenly Ferré felt like a new person, flooded with an awesome yet joyous sense of the presence and power of God. Here was not a dismal end but a new and exciting beginning.

In the face of all "broken things too broke to mend" stands the God who can redeem every human no. Into the threat of personal and global doom and destruction moves the triumphantly risen Jesus of the scars. Only a God with scars can feel and understand the crippling conflicts of our times. From the defeating loneliness which paralyzes people even in the midst of a moving and crawling city to the horrors of armed conflict and war which plague us continually, what kind of a God can speak?—only the One who has for all time conquered the human no.

Who can give courage to those people today seeking refuge in the catacombs of Eastern Europe but the God who himself was once incarcerated in an underground tomb? Who can feel the coughing of a coal miner whose lungs are full of black death and whose children have never known the barest of life's comforts but the risen Christ who knew the pain of rejection, of physical abuse, and excruciating death on the cross?

Who can understand and respond triumphantly to the human no except Jesus, who, through his death and resurrection, gave proof that for all time the human no is not the ultimate end of life? The scars of hate, fear, and bitterness are not the ultimate.

The Christ of the resurrection is neither soft nor plastic. Here is no effeminate Jesus made up like a night club entertainer. Rather, we find a rugged Christ, a Christ of callouses and scars, who holds out his hands and invites us to explore those scars and through the victory of his life, death, and resurrection find the courage and hope to handle those broken things which only appear now to be "too broke to mend."

Never Again to Die

Ernest Campbell

But if we have died with Christ, we believe that we shall also live with him. For we know that Christ being raised from the dead will never die again; death no longer has dominion over him.

(Romans 6:8–9, RSV)

Howard Lowery, when he was President of Wooster College
many years ago, was entertaining Desmond MacCarthy, the
renowned drama critic of the London Sunday *Times* on his
first night in New York City. While it was still light, they
went into a theater to see a play. When the performance was
over they moved out of the theater into the bustling confusion
of Broadway with its dazzling array of blazing lights.
MacCarthy stopped dead still in the middle of the sidewalk,
stared for a long time at the awesome sight, then turned to
his host and said, "Tell me, how do you Americans ever
manage to *really* celebrate anything?"

After all, if we announce the arrival of a new
detergent with a full-page advertisement in the *New York
Times* and an hour-long, prime-time television spectacular,
how do we celebrate the Resurrection? If we hire a band
and pull out all the stops to welcome an eighteen-year-old
guru from the East as he steps out of his silver Rolls Royce,
how do we welcome Jesus back from the dead?

But, for all of our superficial glitter and
grandstanding, our days are not all that different from
earlier times. The living Word always struggles to be heard,
and we struggle to clarify its meaning within the framework
of our needs and experience.

And in our struggle we come to see that there
would be joy at this Easter season if we had nothing more
to celebrate than the memory of a noble life. In these latter
years of the twentieth century we are starved for want of
compelling and worthy examples and models. Disappointment,
disillusionment, and failure have stained our vision of life.

Muckrakers of all sorts seem to delight in exposing the
questionable or seamy sides of our heros and heroines.
We've come to expect the worst and to believe that every
man has his price—it's just a matter of finding it. Cynicism
chokes out our hopes and dreams.

Then we come into confrontation with Jesus
Christ—"Once upon a time there was a man who. . . ."
His life grazes ours like a welcome benediction and the
poison of our bewildered confusion is replaced by a
marvelous healing which gives promise of meaning and
purpose. There is no record that Jesus ever made someone
else sad. He never seemed to hurry, yet he was never late.
He neither bowed to the mighty nor despised the poor. In
fact, Jesus consistently used his powers and gifts for good
and positive ends.

On a trip to Australia a few years ago a good
friend of mine made a remarkably perceptive observation:
Jesus never used the gift of miracle regressively, but always
progressively. For example, he didn't turn wine into water or
bread into stones. In a fit of temper or righteous indignation
he didn't strike Judas with paralysis or blind Pontius Pilate,
and he did not cripple the officers who came to arrest him
that night in the garden. Rather, Jesus had an eye for the
lilies of the field and the birds in the trees. His ears were
tuned to God, and his hands seemed always poised to help
others in their time of need.

And we can all take courage in our day-to-day
confrontation with life in the fact that Jesus spent well over
thirty years walking, thinking, playing, praying, and loving
in a part of our world. I find it enormously reassuring to
realize that he felt my kind of feelings, experienced my kind
of hurts, and laughed and cried even as I do.

The eastern seaboard, which comprises the
original thirteen colonies out of which our great nation has
grown, is dotted with signs that read, "George Washington
Slept Here." Based on the number of such signs, I've

concluded that he spent a great deal of time sleeping. Nevertheless, it seems to do something for American pride and spirit to know that a hero of Washington's political and military accomplishments walked and slept and lived on the very ground we are occupying now.

And in similar fashion I find that my senses are energized by the awareness that Jesus was *here;* he really lived here! As Guinevere remarked after Arthur had left in Tennyson's *Idylls of the King:*

> It was my duty to have loved the highest;
> It surely was my profit had I known;
> It would have been my pleasure had I seen.
> One needs must love the highest when we see it,
> Not Lancelot, nor another.

With nothing more than Jesus' exemplary life to pin our hopes on we could pray devotionally with John Baillie:

> Forbid it, O Father, that the difficulty
> of living well should ever tempt me to fall
> into any kind of heedlessness or despair.
> May I keep it ever in mind that this human
> life was once divinely lived and this world
> once nobly overcome and this body of flesh,
> that now so sorely tries me, once made
> into thy perfect dwelling place.[1]

But that's not all! There would be cause for joy today had we nothing more to celebrate than a noble life that had survived death. Is death the *end* of the road or is it a *bend* in the road? We wonder. In our more optimistic moments we find it easy to affirm the notion that God

---

[1] John Baillie, *A Diary of Private Prayer* (New York: Charles Scribner's Sons, 1952), p. 123.

wouldn't have given birds an instinct to fly south in the
winter if there were no south. So, most of us live with our
hunches and surmises. But if Jesus survived the grave,
possibly . . .

Hear the Good News! Jesus did more than
survive death, he defeated and reversed it! He experienced
death—not somehow, but triumphantly. He was
victorious—irreversibly so. As Paul put it, "We know that
Christ being raised from the dead will never die again;
death no longer has dominion over him." For Israel and for
us, he kept covenant with God—faithful to death. And God
raised him up! His resurrection has about it the ring of a
grand amen—God's "yes" given in answer to all our
wonderment and doubt.

"We know that Christ being raised from the
dead will never die again." Here is *finality* and *inescapability*.
What he achieved in his life and death and rising again needs
neither repetition nor improvement. I like the way Karl
Barth understood it: "It is in the power of the event of
the third day that the event of *the first day* is not something
which belongs to the past, which can be present only by
recollection, tradition, and proclamation, but it is as such
a present event, the event which fills and determines the
whole present." [2]

In the last century there was an uproarious
celebration when America's first transcontinental railroad
was completed. In 1862 and 1864 acts of Congress initiated
the building of this railroad. The Union Pacific Railroad
built westward from Nebraska, and the Central Pacific
Railroad built eastward from California. The two met at
Promontory Point in Utah on May 10, 1869, where a golden
spike was driven into the ground to signal the completion
of this notable endeavor. When that spike was firmly

---

[2] Karl Barth, *Church Dogmatics* (Edinburgh: T. and T. Clark, 1956), vol.
IV, pt. 1, p. 313.

embedded, a telegrapher tapped out this one-word
message . . .

D . . . O . . . N . . . E.

". . . death no longer has dominion over him."
It is D . . . O . . . N . . . E and he ever liveth to make
intercession for us. His sacrifice has power—ample power—
forever.

But there's more! This noble life raised from the
dead destroyed the powers of the present age! Frequently
we have tended to overly personalize the meaning of Christ's
resurrection and have consequently missed to a large degree
its cosmic significance. It is all summed up for us, however—
the individual and corporate meaning of his death and
resurrection—in those assuring words which Paul wrote to
the Christians in Colossae: "And you, who were dead in
trespasses and the uncircumcision of your flesh, God made
alive together with him, having forgiven us all our trespasses,
having canceled the bond which stood against us with its
legal demands; this he set aside, nailing it to the cross" (the
personal aspect). Paul continues, "He disarmed the
principalities and powers and made a public example of them,
triumphing over them in him" (the neglected aspect) (Col.
2:13–15, RSV).

What are these "principalities and powers" Paul
referred to? I believe these have to do with the large,
impersonal forces which strive for control over our lives.
"Principalities and powers" suggest that malevolent network
which the New Testament refers to as "the mystery of
iniquity" (2 Thess. 2:7). The Bible has a way of understanding
our human striving on a much larger board than most of us
project.

Who are the principalities and powers? They
are the states, the system; caste, class, color; frozen
ideologies—either theological or political; codes of

respectability. Anything that in a collective, abstract way moves in to dehumanize people.

The Good News of Easter is that Jesus made short work of the principalities and powers. Against them he was decisively triumphant. Good Friday caused serious questions to be written across that Palestinian sky. As Mennonite John Yoder put it, "There at the cross is the man who loves his enemies, the man whose righteousness is greater than that of the Pharisees, who being rich became poor, who gives his robe to those who took his cloak, who prays for those who despitefully use him." [3]

The question which we must ask in the presence of this awesome scene is whether such values belong to the essence of our life or form an exception that proves the rule. Is that the way life is—loving, giving, serving, dying? The resurrection of Jesus Christ was God's resounding and unalterable "yes."

The principalities and powers are marked for death. That is their fate. The powers have been exposed and condemned. Paul refers to them rather whimsically in his letter to the Corinthians as ". . . the powers-that-be, who soon will be only the powers that have been" (1 Cor. 2:6, Phillips). It was not a *battle* that Jesus won; it was the *war*.

The central claim of the New Testament is not the announcement that a new religion has come into the world. Rather, the central claim of the New Testament is the announcement of the birth of a New World and a New Man. This is why Jesus is called the Last Adam (1 Cor. 15:45). As in the old Adam, all die, even so in the Last Adam shall all be made alive. Adam is synonymous with history. What the Scriptures are declaring is that a new history began with Jesus who was raised from the dead.

I get rather tired of the old history. Just recently

[3] John Howard Yoder, *The Politics of Jesus* (Grand Rapids, MI: Wm. B. Eerdmans Publishing Co., 1972), p. 61.

I heard about an epitaph in an old cemetery in Girard,
Pennsylvania, which reads:

> In memory of
> Ellen Shannon
> Aged 26 years
> Who was fatally burned
> March 21st 1870
> by the explosion of a lamp
> filled with R. E. Danforth's
> Non Explosive
> Burning Fluid [4]

I am tired of nonexplosive fluids exploding; of
fail-proof banks that fail; of sure-fire programs that fall flat.
I'm tired of preventives that don't prevent, of solutions that
do not solve, of remedies that do not cure, of panaceas that
don't pan out. I am tired of promises that aren't kept, of
reforms that change nothing, of gods that smile upon us as
they siphon out our life, of death that masquerades as hope!
In short, I'm tired of Adam.

But that's not the end. Through the resurrection
of Jesus I am filled with living energy and rejoice in Christ—
in whom the old has passed away, and the new has come.

I sometimes think that one reason we are not as
joyful as we ought to be is because we've been overexposed
to the world and underexposed to the gospel. Let this eternal
truth strike us with all of its power: Jesus is conqueror; the
universe is his!

---

[4] Howard F. Lowry, *College Talks* (New York: Oxford University Press,
1969), p. 77.

The Continuation of the Resurrection

Fulton J. Sheen

Therefore, if anyone is in Christ, he is a new creation; the old has passed away. behold the new has come. All this is from God, who through Christ reconciled us to himself and gave us the ministry of reconciliation.

(2 Corinthians 5:17–18, RSV)

The Resurrection and the Crucifixion were never separated by Our Lord. He never spoke of one without the other, for death is the condition of life. The most absurd thing in all the world is the cross by itself. First of all, it symbolizes the basic contradiction of life and death, or love and death. The vertical bar of life, which is upright, is contradicted by the horizontal bar of death, which is prostrate. Even in the psychological order, every complex is a cross, for the libidinous urges of the *id*, in the language of Freud, are contradicted by the social sanction and no-no's of the Superego.

How to resolve the contradiction? By putting Christ on that cross Who will solve the contradiction by making death the condition of life. The week before His Passion, Our Lord told the Greeks: "In truth, in very truth I tell you, a grain of wheat remains a solitary grain unless it falls to the ground and dies; but if it dies, it bears a rich harvest" (John 12:23, NEB). Maybe the Greeks begged Him to go to Athens, the home of wise men. They had killed only one philosopher, and they regretted ever since the hemlock cup they reached to Socrates. If He were speaking to the Jews, He would have quoted the multiple prophecies about the Suffering Servant; but to the Greeks He made nature preach His Gospel. The loneliness and futility of the selfish seed that would stay in its granary here gives way to the "foolishness of the cross," where even life is flung away "as a trinket at one's wrist."

The Resurrection of Christ, like the Incarnation and Passion, is a continuing process. Nothing new is in the world. Only the same old things are happening to new

people, as is proven by "news on the hour." "What plane will
be skyjacked tomorrow?" "Who will be murdered?" Hidden
in the media's love of the tragic is not only a hidden death
wish, but also an unconscious concern with the ultimate:
death. Accidents, muggings, assassinations are interesting as
penultimates because they avoid facing the ultimate. The
same is true of the passion for revolution and the despisal
of the past. One would almost think to hear the revolutionists
speak that they were born without navels—having no debt
or bond or cord to the past. For the first time they no longer
think about history, so as to avoid old errors with new
labels; rather, they seek consciously to create history as a
"now."

But this forgets that what Easter did was to
create the "new." The Church became the "new" Israel,
and man a "new creature." "When anyone is united to
Christ, there is a new world; the old order has gone, and a
new order has already begun" (2 Cor. 5:17, NEB).

The Resurrection, if regarded so exclusively as
past, finds its vision is limited to the empty tomb; if directed
exclusively to the *future*, it zeroes in on judgment and the
final resurrection. But if the Resurrection is progressive,
and based on Christ's victory over death, then it affects me
now. The Resurrection is not just hope in the sense of
futurity, as Ernest Bloch would have us believe. Oscar
Wilde's remark is here apropos that a world map which fails
to display the land of Utopia hardly deserves a glance. Nor
is credence to be put in Bultmann's view which ignores
the historical part of the Resurrection and makes it only
mythological or subjective. According to Bultmann what
matters is the "now," not whether Christ really rose from
the dead. Nor may one so eliminate the future and the
transcendent as does Feuerbach, who would "transform
theologians into anthropologists, lovers of God into lovers
of man, candidates for the next world into students of this

world, religious and earthly monarchs and lords into free, self-reliant citizens of earth."

Nowhere in Scripture does belief in the Resurrection as a fact and as a hope militate against responsibility to earth, but rather "brings healing for all mankind" and demands "living a life of temperance, honesty and godliness in the present age" (Titus 2:11–14, NEB). The Christian is one who simultaneously rejoices in hope and endures affliction: "Let hope keep you joyful; in trouble stand firm; persist in prayer" (Rom. 12:12, NEB).

The Resurrection is not just something that happened; it is something still happening. And it continues because it happened once, like a great cosmic explosion that sent the planets spinning and in constant motion.

The Resurrection Begins with the Cross

The mystery begins not with the empty tomb, but with Calvary. The message of the angels brought their minds back to this fact: "Fear nothing; you are looking for Jesus of Nazareth, who was crucified" (Mark 16:6, NEB). St. Peter stressed the same Death-Life connection: "You used heathen men to crucify and kill him. But God raised him to life again" (Acts 2:23, NEB). The Easter problem is not, do dead men rise? But does The Crucified Man rise? The conviction of the Risen Christ comes not just from the fact of the empty tomb: "Why search among the dead for one who lives?" (Luke 24:5, NEB). The empty tomb did not convince the women who brought spices, nor Magdalene who thought the Body had been taken away, nor Peter and James who thought the story was a "woman's tale," nor Thomas who refused the testimony of witnesses, nor the soldiers who were present at the emptying. The Cross that redeemed us from sin solves the mystery of the tomb. Nor did Christ appear to Pilate or Herod or Judas, but He did

appear to those who knew Him in His death in some way.
Each came to know Him by a gesture familiar to Him:
Magdalene by His voice, the seven disciples by the
miraculous catch of fish, the disciples of Emmaus by the
breaking of the Bread, and Thomas by the scars. Even Paul
who had a vision of the Glorified Christ saw Him inseparably
from the ongoing Crucifixion: "Why do you persecute Me?"
As death was His penalty for our sinfulness, so the
Resurrection was the sign of our forgiveness. The Cross
was man's judgment of Christ; the empty tomb was God's
judgment of Christ. *No one really ever sees that the tomb
is empty and Christ is risen except from the scaffolding of
the Cross.* "The God of our fathers raised up Jesus whom
you had done to death by hanging him on a gibbet" (Acts
5 : 30, NEB). If there had been no sunset, there would be no
sunrise. Will the sunrise convince the blind man unless he
has had some knowledge of light? Only he who has been
inwardly touched by His Word will ever be persuaded He
broke the bonds of death. Out of the cloud, the sun; out of
the earth, the bud; out of the clod, the green; and out of the
grave, our forgiveness.

Physical Easter

If we were conscious in the darkness of the
womb, would we not have shrunk to have left its security for
an unknown life? If some agnostic could have addressed us
he might have said: "Do you really believe there is another
life than prenatal life? What evidence have you who live in
darkness that there is such a thing as light? Why barter away
the security of nourishment without effort for the
insecurity of 'pie in the sky'? You may have faith that there
is another world than the one you experience, but your faith
is subjective and so void of any scientific certitude of
another life."

But would we not have answered: "Listen!

See these arms of mine laid across my breast, with fingers at their tips? Would I have ever formed them unless I could touch something and hold somebody like myself? My eyes have a capacity for seeing, my ears for hearing, though I never saw a sun or heard a symphony. My legs! Useless they are now, but were they not made for playing, for walking, for running? I am made for another world, even though my senses have never seen it. Some day the particle of flesh which entombs me will burst with a momentary cry of Calvary's agony of birth and then will come the joy of light and music and friendship: 'A woman in labour is in pain because her time has come; but when the child is born she forgets the anguish in her joy that a man has been born into the world' " (John 16:21, NEB). The exactitude of our Lord's language—"anguish" and "joy"—means that present groanings are but creating within us a larger capacity for joy. "Our troubles are slight and short-lived; and their outcome an eternal glory which outweighs them far" (2 Cor. 4:17, NEB).

Spiritual Easter

When a man is born, he is now confronted with the possibility of another birth. He can stay in the womb of nature, or he can undergo a momentary death and rise to the life of the spirit. The travail pangs of "mortification" are the precursors of joys. There must be *fellowship* with the sufferings of Christ before we can share His glory: "We are God's heirs and Christ's fellow-heirs, if we share his sufferings now in order to share his splendour hereafter" (Rom. 8:17, NEB). This was the problem of Nicodemus. When the Lord told him that he had to be reborn, the old lawyer asked: "But how is it possible for a man to be born when he is old?" (John 3:5). Some are dull to the things of the Spirit: "A man who is unspiritual refuses what belongs to the Spirit of God; it is folly to him; he cannot grasp it . . ." (1 Cor. 2:14, NEB). Dr. Nicodemus, the intellectual,

could not conceive of eggs hatching or of men becoming
Christians.

Humanity is made up of two kinds of men: the
"once-born" and the "twice-born"—the once-born who left
a tomb of flesh with a cry, and the twice-born who are
"born of God" and made partakers not only of the nature
of their parents, but of the nature of God. Physical birth is
the coming into a natural environment for which it has been
created; spiritual birth is the coming into the spiritual
environment. As Browning put it: "Though He is so bright
and we so dim, we are made in His image to witness to Him."

But a man cannot be coerced into spiritual
relationship; it demands consent and must be self-determined.
This second birth is more flesh-shattering and catastrophic
than the first, and more umbilical cords are broken than in
seeing the light of day. If a block of marble bloomed, that
would be something beyond its nature and capacity, and if
the man of flesh becomes a spiritual man, this is the kind of
birth that demands not only the services of the Divine
Obstetrician, but also the will to "die" on the part of the
fetus. First is the dying to self in union with the Cross, then
the Easter of an inner peace nothing can shatter.

Like the fetus in the womb, the humanist might
say to himself: would I have this intellect which can know
the truths of geography and the truths of astrophysics if it
were not made to know Truth itself? If my heart can thrill
to human love which never completely satisfies, does not
this mean that I was made for a "Love we fall just short of
in all love"? If I want life not for seven more minutes, nor
seven more years, but enduring life, does it not mean that
somewhere there must be a Life that is not mingled with its
shadow, death; a Truth that is not mingled with its shadow,
doubt; and a Love that is not spoiled with its shadow, hate?
Is this not Pure Life, Pure Truth, Pure Love with Father,
Son and Holy Spirit?

But before I can attain it, I must hear: "If anyone

wishes to be a follower of mine, he must leave self behind;
he must take up his cross and come with me" (Matt. 16:24,
NEB). But the cross is no self-mutilation or masochism. It is
a plucking off of dead buds that the new buds may blossom;
it is the pruning of a tree for a richer harvest; it is the dull
rehearsal for the triumph of a concert. *God is not the God
of dead things, but of renewed things. He does not change
the ideal to fit the way men live; but He changes the way
men live to give them the ideal.* Only he who elects to live
for himself remains in the tomb. No self-denial is ever
without a resurrection of the spirit; in each new-born soul
there is verified: "Now at the place where he had been
crucified, there was a garden . . ." (John 19:41, NEB).

The Womb of Death

The last womb through which we pass is the
womb of Time to give birth to eternity. Death is the last
penalty for sin; it is the Golgotha that individualizes us
regardless of how conformist we were in life. Here we step
out of the ranks as our name is called; a line is drawn beneath
the sum of days and that is the computer slip we carry to
judgment. During life many of our decisions were imperfect
because flesh, time, and a momentary advantage confused
the issue. But when the bird is released from the cage, it flies;
so at death the wings of the spirit of man in the light of his
previous graces make the ultimate and final decision of being
for or against Christ.

"I believe in the Resurrection of the body" is
the Easter that the person looks forward to after his last
breath on the cross of life. St. Paul in 1 Corinthians 15:35–50
resorts to the Lord's analogy of the seed. The seed that is
planted in the ground does not rise with the same body that
was buried. The new one is quite different, though definitely
related to it. The Easter of the divinized-man is not just the
reward of an immortal soul. The Resurrection is not

soul-salvation, but person-salvation. Since Christ the Head of a regenerated Body rose, then the members are ontologically bound up with His Resurrection: "But the truth is, Christ was raised to life—the firstfruits of the harvest of the dead" (1 Cor. 15:20, NEB). The ancient Jewish law obliged the farmer to bring the first fruit of his harvest and "wave it before the Lord" as a token that the whole field and the farmer himself belonged to God. Christ is that "first fruit" of our humanity. With all our failings, we are dedicated to Him in our prayers, our works, our sicknesses and our joys. Our resurrection is assured though it does require the last configuration Christ, sharing in His Death to share in His Glory. As we might have shrunk from breaking the umbilical cord, so we shrink from shattering the cords of time. Christ came not to negate life, but to give it more abundantly. Anyone who ever denied himself a theft or an adultery has already placed death in the middle of his life as the condition of peace of conscience. All such acts stem not from our instinct of life, but from our wisdom of death. "Christ leads me through no darker rooms than He has gone before."

Resurrection of the Body

"It is not true that the body is for lust; it is for the Lord, and the Lord for the body" (1 Cor. 6:13, NEB).

Because the body was not made for drugs, alcoholism, fornication, and perversity, but for the Lord, it must be raised from the dead. Sickness and sin are obstacles that hinder man in his path toward full humanity in Christ Jesus. Addiction, illness, and carnality are limitations on a life created by God; they are a sign of the chaos that muddles and muddies bodies until the stone is rolled away from their sepulcher. He who has worked with addicts has seen a thousand angels singing over empty tombs: "See the place where they laid Him." With a deep pastoral sense, he avoids two extremes: not of seeing the delinquent as alien to society, nor, on the other hand, of manifesting a superiority over those who have fallen.

In Florence is the statue made for the tomb of Pope Julius by Michelangelo. Four figures are struggling, wrestling, straining to emerge from the cold inert marble. Effort and pain are written on their muscles and faces as they strive for triumph, from non-being to being, from chaos to form. The person who has lifted an alcoholic or addict from the pit and translated him to the newness of life has contemporized the empty tomb. But he has done something also for himself: "Any man who brings a sinner back from his crooked ways will be rescuing his soul from death and cancelling innumerable sins" (James 5:20, NEB).

Resurrection of Minds

Soldiers of habit may station themselves at the tombs of the depressed, the defeated, and the crucified, but they give way to the superior power of angels, asking, "Why seek you the living among the dead?" The tragedy of the mentally troubled is that so many disbelieve in their having an Easter as Peter did, calling it a "woman's tale." The mentally crucified are in a condition of broken relationships from want of intimacy. Jung said that every neurotic has a religious problem, for the illness is concerned with ultimates, such as destiny, realities, value, God: as Dr. Harry Stack Sullivan wrote, "As long as the individual in an acutely disturbed state is busy shouting about being God, he does not have time to be aware of the fact that he is puny, mortal, and scared to death."

The mentally sick have a sense of shut-up-ness and shut-out-ness, or in Scriptural language of being "outside the Camp" of the people of God. So often they feel forsaken of God. In this condition they often feel that the last person

who should come to their relief is a man of God. They repeat
the demonic cry of the Gospel: "You Son of God, what do
you want with us? Have you come here to torment us before
our time?" (Matt. 8:29, NEB).

The Lord never took away from His Church
the power of raising up from the tomb such tortured souls.
As one travels the country, one wonders if the superior
type of priest among all the services of the Church is not to
be found among those who minister to the mentally
handicapped and the deeply troubled. In other forms of
ministry, love is often reciprocated; in the care of the
mentally distressed, the chaplain's love, so often
unreciprocated, takes on the character of the *Agapé* of
Christ Himself. Some of them may not be skilled in
psychological techniques, but they often produce more
mental resurrections than technicians. Consider the
depression of Beethoven when at the age of thirty-one he
became deaf. In despair he resolved to kill himself for never
having heard the Ninth Symphony or the *Missa Solemnis*.
Then came one who believed in the Resurrection and
changed his attitude: "How beautiful life is. The Kingdom
of God is within." Then came the exultant triumphs of the
Eroica Symphony, the Third, Fifth, and Seventh, which
verified the Resurrection theme of Paul: "No wonder we
do not lose heart! Though our outward humanity is in
decay, yet day by day we are inwardly renewed" (2 Cor.
4:16, NEB).

A priest gave a retreat in a large security prison.
On the way to the platform to address the inmates, he
slapped one of them on the back: "Gee, you're a handsome
guy." Inquiry later on revealed that his mind had the same
pallor as his skin: depressed, and helpless. But let him tell
the story of his resurrection, through the "Great Flea."

"I was like a flea floating down a river on a
matchstick, enjoying what I thought was life. When the
water got rough, I hung on a little tighter repeating, 'It'll

pass!' When the water was running smooth, I dabbled my
feet and gathered a few other fleas upon my stick (a family).
I was especially happy when the river was full of splinters
and other fleas passed near. I joined them in talk, in song.
Sometimes I kept them so long, sometimes we enjoyed each
other's company so well, they forgot their destinations. I
did not forget. I never had one. I never looked for one.
When my little canoe hit rainy weather, I took my little
fleas on board and unloaded them to a stick with more shelter
and, as nice and as slow you please, began to pail out the
water that threatened. Many times friendly fleas saw I was
struggling to stay afloat, they grabbed their pails—after all,
what's fleaship for? I went along like that, never kicking.
I thought life is too sweet. Then I hit my iceberg—my
Lusitania went down! Yes, I could swim. The friendly fleas
did all they could to save my stick. It was hopeless!! I swam
and made it to this little island. It was not deserted; in fact,
it's a place where all the torpedoed fleas gather. A place to
rebuild a new stick and get back into the swim of things.
I've busied myself on this little isle hastily putting pieces
together, driving a nail, slapping a coat of paint (a lot of
outside work). Yes, I have something now that will float
(how long?). I'm not sure, I wanta catch up!

"Now last week I meet an extraordinarily Grand
Flea, a sailor who did not go down, whose job it is to patrol
the river stopping at all these little isles; helping all the
stranded; giving tools, provisions, but most of all advice.
Some fleas listen, some fleas go on ahead fixing their new
splinters. I always liked a good story (time out for a ball
game was never my problem), so I pulls up a grain of sand.
The Admiral walks right up to me and says, 'You got a nice
face for a flea.' His flattery wins me. I'm listening to
whatever he says now. (Inside my heart tells me it's more
than just that.) This Navigator has a million tales; tells us
about a place up the river—Jordan-burg. He says it's the
home of his Boss. It's a beautiful layout. Everybody's

welcome. The Boss wants you to bring friends if you can—the-more-the-merrier type of guy. You get a choice where you want to live, in His Father's House, the Son's or the Holy Ghost's. They have so many vacancies, must be three Grand Hotels? I want to go there. I listened real close, didn't want to miss any tips. He talked about the river as one life, using it as a tool to get to the Boss's Place. I learned life is not to folly or dip in the water. It's the purpose to reach real life—Jordan-town. So I'm turned on, tuned in and my ship needs a few more necessities. I'm working on them now. I'll catch you on the Rib-ber!!! (That's what happened to me.)"

Resurrection of the Spirit

There had to be a Resurrection, otherwise there would be no pattern for the body turning from its own lust to become a temple of God, or for a broken mind, like Anton T. Boisen's, eventually becoming the source of consolation, hope and mental reunification to thousands in the same hospital where he had been a patient. In his *Exploration of the Inner World*, he wrote: "Instead of allowing the psychiatrist to remain the exclusive keeper of the lower regions, I am hoping and laboring for the day when the specialists in religion will be able with his help to go down to the depths of the grim abyss after those who are capable of responding, those in whom some better self is seeking to come to birth."

Beyond both of these is the resurrection of the spirit, like St. Francis who rose from the tomb of wealth to the newness of a life of poverty; or like St. Augustine, the "hippie" university student, who was dead to the spirit and then walked on the wings of faith; or Lydia, the dyer of purple, whose home became the center for the evangelization of Europe. Michelangelo believed that in every block of marble was a figure yearning to be born. Viktor Frankl, from a psychiatric point of view, teaches that the repression of this spiritual birth is "the real pathology of our age." Carl Jung adds: "About one-third of my cases are not suffering from any clinically definable neurosis, but from the senselessness and aimlessness of their lives." It is the boredom of living in tombs without a regeneration which is the general neurosis of our times.

Modernized, the Easter message means that God recycles human garbage. He can turn prostitutes like Magdalene into disciples, broken reeds like Simon Peter into rocks, and political-minded Simon Zealots into martyrs for the faith. *God is the God of the Second Chance.* What the Resurrection does for the unhatched eggs of humanity is to make life adventurous. Up until the new life comes to them, they are bounded by the cosmic, the human, and the grave. Their life is like a detective story, the full meaning of which is hidden until the last line when one discovers that "the butler did it." The plane of life is boarded, but one has no clear idea where it is going until the moment of landing. The spirit, on the contrary, renewed by conversion, knows the end and the beginning. Like the great classical writers such as Homer and Shakespeare, the point of the story is told at the beginning, so unlike detective stories. Life then becomes like a storm at sea which is made the more interesting because of the certitude given that one will arrive safely at a port. One may not know when life will end, but that only heightens the watchfulness and inspires one to keep oil in the lamp; no one knows the hour of the coming of the Bridegroom. Unresurrected lives are like a man who spent his life in prison, not knowing that the door was open; he never tried it. When this life is only the penultimate there is a thrill in working toward the ultimate. How different when life is bounded by a search for an object which is abandoned when it no longer gives pleasure, and one must seek a new object. Dilettante minds plant idealism one month, then pull up the tender roots to

plant realism; then sow existentialism only to abort it; they
discover in the end that there is no harvest.

       When a person is raised up from his own
dead past to a goodness which in terms of the past cannot be
accounted for, he is face to face with the miracle of the
Creed: "I believe in the Resurrection." Or when a man is
able to take the worst the world can give, and make it
contribute to his spiritual growth, he has modernized the
miracle of the seed "which is the Word." As Bonhoeffer
wrote in his prison: "Who am I? They mock me, these
lovely questions of mind. Whoever I am, Thou knowest,
O God, I am Thine." The only ones who suffer from the
problem of identity are those who have no goal, no destiny,
no eternal shore. How do we know the identity of the
State of New York? By its boundaries. How do we know
the identity of a baseball diamond? By its foul lines.
How do we know our identity? By limits, by laws, by
destinies, by God. Once the Good Friday–Easter Sunday
syndrome is made the rule of life, then one sees that only the
Christ-fettered are free.

An Endless Tryst

James Armstrong

*For I am sure that neither death, nor life,
nor angels, nor principalities, nor things
present, nor things to come, nor powers,
nor height, nor depth, nor anything else
in all creation, will be able to separate
us from the love of God in Christ Jesus
our Lord.*

(Romans 8:38, RSV)

Two hundred miles northeast of Los Angeles is a baked-out gorge called Death Valley—the lowest place in the United States, dropping 276 feet below sea level. It is also the hottest place in the country, with an official recording of 134 degrees. Streams flow into Death Valley only to disappear, and a scant two and a half inches of rain falls on the barren wasteland each year.

But, some time ago, an amazing thing happened. For nineteen straight days rain fell onto that bone-dry earth. Suddenly all kinds of seed, dormant for years, burst into bloom. In a valley of death there was life!

That is the Easter message. A desert becomes a garden. Beauty transcends the ugly. Love outwits and outlasts hatred. A tomb is emptied. The grim and haunting outline of a cross disappears in the glow of Easter morn.

But more . . .

The Easter story deals with the fact of our mortality. We are finite creatures, made of clay, here today and gone tomorrow. At the very moment of birth we begin the slow process that leads toward death.

Easter assures us that death can be faced squarely.

We haven't always done that, you know.

A little girl next door asks if bugs eat dead people when they are buried in the earth. You try to explain the meaning of death with faith and dignity. She seems to grasp something of what you are saying. Later an irate mother confronts you and asks, "What do you mean by talking to my daughter about death? She's much too young for that." The child is not too young to ask; just too young for an honest, searching response.

A woman is suffering from an incurable disease. Her physician discovers the nature of her illness and tells her husband. They mustn't let her in on their secret. They must spare her feelings. No need to add greater burden to her pain. The fact is, she already senses the truth. But because of a mutual fear, she hesitates to mention it; her husband won't talk about it; her doctor says nothing. They play this sad game of make-believe and forfeit the chance to share one of life's most meaningful experiences.

Thank God for people like Raymond A. Moody and for books like *Life after Life* and *Death and Dying* that are helping those of us who profess to believe in a Christian interpretation of things to accept the reality of death as the natural consequence of everything that goes before.

It is appointed unto us—every single one of us— once to die. That knowledge may intimidate us; may cause us to feel a bit squeamish. After all, it rings down the curtain on the familiar and thrusts us into the realm of the mysterious unknown. As we grow older we adjust to its reality; given a particular set of circumstances we may even welcome it. But, however we prepare for and relate to death, it remains mysterious and unknown.

Thus, the importance of Jesus of Nazareth. *Not only is he the Lord of life—all of life; he is the interpreter and conqueror of death.*

Easter is not a fanciful myth unrelated to the here and now. Rather, its truth is bound up with the most profound levels of our present experience.

I don't understand the Resurrection. I can't dissect and analyze it as a scientist deals with quantitative judgments in a laboratory. But, I believe in it! The record can be called into question. Paul and other convinced witnesses can be challenged. But their words were not erased; were not denied. In writing the church in Corinth,

the Apostle said five hundred persons had seen—had literally
seen—the risen One. How or where we do not know, but
Paul dared anyone to challenge their testimony. It stood.
He went on to say that if Christ is not risen our faith is in
vain. The entire gospel story was written against the backdrop
of the Resurrection. It was a *living* Christ who brought the
church into being—and who is able to touch and transform
our lives even now. Something happened that first Easter
day, something that turned a band of wavering, grief-stricken
mortals into the convinced and passionate messengers of a
new, life-giving word.

    Yes—the Christian faith enables us to face death
squarely. I don't know what the word *heaven* denotes.
Surely it has nothing to do with golden streets or pearly gates
or static bliss. Marc Connelly's *Green Pastures* was a
fascinating fable; nothing else. Floating clouds and angel
wings and endless fish fries (or other forms of sensuous
delight) have nothing to do with an extension of life beyond
the grave. Eternity does more than push out the borders of
time; heaven is not a geographical spot "up yonder."

    *Eternal life, whatever else it may be, is
relationship*. It suggests an endless trysting place where
God and the personal dimension of his creation are bound
together.

    Short hours before Jesus was dragged through the
streets of Jerusalem to his death, he met with his closest
friends. "I am in my Father and you are in me and I in you,"
he said. That is relationship.

    He said, "I leave the world and go to the Father."
That is relationship.

    He said, "I go to prepare a place for you . . .
where I am there you may be also." That speaks of
relationship.

    Nor is this solely a relationship between God
and the individual. To use a quaint old phrase, we are

surrounded by "a cloud of witnesses." We say we believe in
"the communion of the saints." An endless trysting place
suggests not only relationship, but interrelationship.

This is one of the meanings of the Transfiguration. In a moment of high inspiration Moses and
Elijah appeared out of the past to Jesus. The three
communed. The past was linked with the present and the
dead and living inhabited the same realm. No H. G. Wells's
"time machine" was involved; no Houdini's magic. Rather,
it was the compression of the ages in one remarkable moment
of conscious time.

Last month I visited the widow of an older
friend. He had died in February. The pain was fresh and raw.
Yet, she was a woman of remarkable faith. She remembered
a conversation they had had ten days before Earl's death.
He knew he was going. He looked up, smiled and said,
"Will you send me some mail?"

She asked, "Who will deliver it?"

"Oh," he said, "we'll have more and more
friends coming that way." The "cloud of witnesses. . . ."

My mother died three years ago. She was in her
mid-eighties and had lived a full and generous life. Hers was
a courageous faith. I phoned her when she was about to
enter the hospital for surgery. We all knew she was
suffering from an advanced malignancy. "Are you afraid?"
I asked. "No," she said. "My mother went like this, my
brother went like this; hundreds of thousands of people go
like this every year. If they can do it I guess I can."

Although we were separated by more than a
thousand miles I was able to be with her twice during the
final weeks of her life. When she died I flew to southern
California to join my sister for a last farewell. While there
I went to the hospital to thank one particular shift of nurses—
in the intensive care unit—for their beautiful tenderness in
caring for mother. I thanked the head nurse, who responded
with an unexpected word. She told me that during one of

my visits with mother two of her nurses had been working with a patient on the other side of the curtain from where mother and I were talking. Suddenly they left the patient, went to a far corner of the ward, wept, and quietly embraced. One asked, "Have you ever heard anything more beautiful?"

I don't know what conversation they could have been referring to. Mother was too weak for us to talk very much and the situation didn't call for words. As I think back, I do remember one vivid but brief exchange. I was holding her hand and she smiled and said, "It's all right, Jim. I have more people over there waiting for me than I have here to say good-bye to." Those may have been the words that prompted the response.

Do you recall Wordsworth's poem "We are Seven"? A little girl is telling the poet about her family. Two are at Conway, two at the sea, and then herself. "But, that's only five," says the poet. The eight-year-old smiles and replies, "The other two are in the churchyard just twelve steps from our door." Then follow these words:

> "But they are dead; those two are dead!
> Their spirits are in heaven!"
> 'Twas throwing words away; for still
> The little Maid would have her will,
> And say, "Nay, we are seven."

The "cloud of witnesses" from another perspective.

All this may seem overly sentimental to those concerned with "macho" images; overly simplistic to those impressed by what they might call "logic" or "reason." But, dismiss the testimony of the faithful as we will, the *fact* remains: their lives are immeasurably enriched by a quality of experience and relationship that has escaped most of us; their lives are energized by a Spirit that is a total stranger to most of us; they have found a depth of being and an inner strength that has eluded most of us.

Lest you feel this endless tryst is an updating of "pie in the sky bye and bye," let me add a further word. Before dawn on January 20, 1979, in a suburb of San Salvador, uniformed agents of El Salvador's dictator Carlos Humberto Romero burst into a Roman Catholic retreat center and sprayed the area with machine-gun fire. Four young people and a thirty-one-year-old priest were killed. More than thirty others, most of them in their teens, were arrested, interrogated, and charged with "subversive acts." No one was armed. No resistance was offered. The people had just been sleeping.

The following day heroic Archbishop Oscar Romero spoke at a Requiem Mass. More than one hundred priests celebrated the Mass with him. An estimated 25,000 people gathered on the church steps and spilled out onto the public square. The indignant archbishop, who labeled the government's account of the event "a lie from start to finish," called Father Ortiz, the priest killed, "a murder victim *who speaks to us of the resurrection.*"

You see—the resurrection story is not sentimental; it is not simplistic. It deals with fundamental issues of freedom and justice, with life and death in a broader perspective.

Awhile ago I stated that Jesus of Nazareth is the Lord of life—*all* of life. And he is. But our ways and values are so alien to his.

We strut and preen, are proud and vain. And he said, "Blessed are the poor in spirit."

We apply cosmetics, pretend and say, "Doesn't he look natural." We purchase gaudy funerals and relegate death to an unreal zone of silence. And he said, "Blessed are they that mourn."

We boast and brag; we gloat over the substance and nature of our conquests. And he said, "Blessed are the meek."

We know the meanings of selfishness and corruption and immorality, of undisciplined habits and relationships in our daily lives. And he said, "Blessed are those who hunger and thirst after righteousness."

We are jealous, bitter, vengeful, unforgiving. And he said, "Blessed are the merciful."

We misuse and exploit persons we say we love. We are often driven by senses gone wild. And he said, "Blessed are the pure in heart."

We play war games with instruments of war; deal out weapons of destruction to almost every hostile nation on the face of the globe; base an economy on the profits of war. We rely upon violence to solve our problems. And he said, "Blessed are the peacemakers."

We curb our bets, play it safe, refuse to run risks or stand up for those ideals we somehow know are valid and true. And he said, "Blessed are they who are persecuted for righteousness' sake. . . . Blessed are *you* when you are reviled and persecuted . . . for my sake." That's the way it's always been with persons of integrity.

The Christ *is* the Lord of all of life and to deny him is, in a sense, to crucify him on our terms and in our ways. But at this sacred season we need to move beyond betrayal to affirmation, beyond our weakness to his strength, beyond death to life.

There is more to life than life as we experience it. We must never minimize the joys, privileges, and demands of the here and now. But, beyond the immediacy of this moment and the prospects of this world, there is a further dimension of reality.

The Apostle summed it up:

> I am convinced that there is nothing in death
> or life, in the realm of spirits or superhuman
> powers, in the world as it is or the world as it
> shall be, in the forces of the universe, in heights
> or depths—nothing in all creation that can separate
> us from the love of God in Christ Jesus
> our Lord (Rom. 8:38, NEB).

God's Protest against Death and God's Celebration of Freedom

Jürgen Moltmann

And when our mortality has been clothed with immortality, then the saying of Scripture will come true: "Death is swallowed up; victory is won." "O Death, where is your victory? O Death, where is your sting?" The sting of death is sin, and sin gains its power from the law; but, God be praised, he gives us the victory through our Lord Jesus Christ.

(1 Corinthians 15:54–57, NEB)

"Death is swallowed up in victory.
 O death, where is thy victory?
 O death, where is thy sting?"
The sting of death is sin, and the power of sin is the law.
But thanks be to God, who gives us the victory through our
Lord Jesus Christ (1 Cor. 15:55–57, RSV).

In these unforgettable words Paul celebrates the victory
of life over death and sin, which make life in this world
into a hell. But it isn't easy for us to repeat or affirm this
hymn of freedom.

    "I'm living among middle-class English people,"
said a participant of the Accra ecumenical conference in 1974,
"who have a good education, beautiful houses, a secure
income, and generally a happy family life. Their hope is
that society will stay as it used to be." In today's economic
crisis, however, their hope is giving way to profound
cynicism: "Life has no meaning, and anyone who claims
that it does is either a fool who can't see how things really
are, or a scoundrel who is exploiting human credulity for his
own ends."

    "Can we celebrate life in the midst of death?"
asks an Argentinian friend in a 1978 Christmas letter. "For
those of us who live on this vast Latin American continent
and who try to spread the witness of Jesus Christ here, this
question is not just an idle phrase. Death surrounds us here
not only in the form of subversive violence and repressive
measures which claim victims daily, but death also surrounds
us in a much more insidious and cruel form—rising
unemployment, a drop of real income, and growing child

mortality rates." One must ask, can we really celebrate the
victory of the risen Christ, or should we not lament the
triumph of Pilate and all the tyrants who have followed him?

Cynicism and Despair

In the affluent "first world," many people today
are becoming cynical and narrow-minded. They close their
eyes so as not to see the misery of the Third World. They
cover their ears and try not to hear the "voice from the
depths." They just want to keep what they have. And yet
they feel deeply just how meaningless their lives are.

In the terror of the Third World, people are
driven to despair. They see violent death every day; they are
suppressed. They cry out and then become apathetic because
no one hears them.

Both experiences seem to deny the resurrection
of Christ. Victory seems swallowed up by death, and hell
triumphs—not just in the next life, but here in this life
through the systematic use of torture on a massive scale
in many countries.

From the perspective of history and experience,
Easter is absurd. It cannot be proved, for in the context of
history death reigns supreme. Paul, too, in his lifetime, saw
more crosses and experienced more persecution than Easter
experiences. But if we can learn, like Paul and the first
witnesses of Easter, to see ordinary reality in the light of
the resurrection of Christ, things look quite different, for
then the inevitability of violence and death is absurd. Nothing
is inevitable. Nothing has to be accepted blindly.

Faith then means not only belief in the truth of
Christ's resurrection and the hope of life after death; it
means above all standing up and sharing in the creative
power of God which makes the impossible possible and
calls into being things which are not yet in existence

(Rom. 4:17). The faith of Easter makes us realize that the resurrection of the crucified Christ from the dead is our great alternative to death in this world. It means seeing Christ's resurrection as God's passionate love for the lives of those threatened by and with death. It means sharing in this loving protest, shaking off the apathy of resignation and the cynicism of affluence and struggling against the henchmen of death.

When Christians have disregarded this critical and liberating power of Easter, as they have done often enough in the past, their faith has degenerated into safe belief in verifiable facts and a barren hope in the life hereafter, as if death were simply a fate to be endured at the end of life. Yet the evil power of death is present in the midst of life: in the economic death of those who are left to starve, the political death of the oppressed, the social death of the handicapped, the screaming death of napalm bombs and torture, the silent death of the resigned soul.

Belief in the resurrection is not confirmed through historical proofs, or reserved for the life hereafter; it is confirmed here and now through the courage to rebel, through protest against the powers of death, and through one's devotion to the victory of life.

Victory of Life

We can't speak convincingly of Christ's resurrection unless we share in the movement of the Spirit, "which is poured out on all flesh" to make it live. This movement of the Spirit is God's "liberation movement," because it is the process by which the world is created anew. Resurrection means, therefore, that we must be reborn out of our powerlessness and apathy into "living hope." And "living hope" these days implies passionate commitment to life and living protest against death. If we fail to dispute

the power of the rulers of this world, we shall never attain
to the certainty that in the end death will be swallowed up
in victory.

The resurrection is a hope which can only be
understood in terms of the cross—that is, to stay in the
struggle of love against death. That is why the Swiss pastor
Kurt Marti wrote:

> It could happen this way to many men...
> but there comes a resurrection
> which is different, quite different than we thought.
> There comes a resurrection which is
> the rebellion of God against the masters,
> and against the master of the masters—death.

With Christ's resurrection God's revolution
began. It continues in the spirit of hope and will be
accomplished when, along with death, all "powers and
principalities" are finally done away with (1 Cor. 15:28).

The hope of resurrection finds human
expression in the protest against death and its henchmen.
But it is fed and sustained by something else—the joyful
abundance of God's future. The freedom granted by the
hope of resurrection is expressed in the struggle against all
the forces that outwardly or inwardly deny life. But it
does not live on protest; rather it is sustained by joy in the
coming victory of life. The argument the Apostle repeatedly
uses when he is speaking not of deliverance of sin, law, and
death, but of freedom for life, justice, and glory, is "how
much more shall God give?" (cf. Heb. 9:14, Matt. 7:11).

We might call this the "surplus value of hope."
It is the "extra" that the resurrection of Christ adds to the
forces of liberation, "nevertheless" with which we resist
evil. Our own resignation is simply the reverse side of the
"how much longer?" of hope which inspires us. Our protest
and struggles are grounded in this hope, otherwise they are

nothing more than accusations and campaigns of revenge. But greater hope must come alive in such protest and struggle, or else they become religious seduction.

Feast of Freedom

Where does the "surplus value" of hope come alive and how do we experience it? Easter is a celebration; it is a celebration of freedom. The laughter of the redeemed, the dancing of the liberated, the creative play of the imagination begin at Easter. Easter hymns from time immemorial have rejoiced in the victory of life by laughing at death, mocking hell, ridiculing the mighty who spread fear and terror around them. Easter sermons used to begin with a good joke. "Make a man laugh and you open heaven to him," goes a rabbinical proverb.

Easter is a liberating celebration. Wherever it is celebrated people must eat and drink. One can't really celebrate the Resurrection without the Eucharist. The Last Supper creates fellowship with the hungry and thirsty. So in order to discover the new fellowship we must invite everyone to share our bread. The same is true on a world-wide scale. Easter celebrations in the "first world" are really not celebrations at all because we fail to share the burden of the hungry people of the world. Celebrations should not go on behind closed and locked doors.

Easter is the celebration of freedom. It makes the life it touches into a life of celebration. "The risen Christ makes life into a constant celebration," Athanasius writes. But can all of life be a celebration, including the shadowy sides of death, guilt, and senseless suffering? Yes, I believe so. When we realize that the celebration is led by the rejected, suffering, crucified Son of man from Nazareth, then every "no" is consumed in this deep "yes" and destroyed by its victory.

Easter is the *protest of God* against death and the

celebration of freedom from death. If we fail to keep the two together, we cannot understand the resurrection of the crucified Christ. Struggle is the protest of the hopeful, and hope is the celebration of those who struggle.

> Whoever makes someone laugh
> opens heaven to him.
> Whoever gives someone patience
> opens the future for him
> Whoever accepts someone
> as he himself is
> accepted by Christ
> enables that person to sing in praise of life.

> Let us depart
> from our habits
> and learn hope from the Bible.
> Let us depart
> and cross the border
> and inject life with hope.
> Let us no longer respect borders,
> but rather the One who opens borders.
> He is risen.
> Jesus is truly risen.
> The Lord be praised forever.
> Amen.

Christ the Lord

Robert A. Raines

Just as day was breaking, Jesus stood on the beach; yet the disciples did not know that it was Jesus.

(John 21:4, RSV)

It is striking that in most of the Resurrection stories Jesus appears to his disciples incognito at first—the stranger on the road to Emmaus . . . the man Mary thought was the gardener . . . the one who appeared in the Upper Room . . . the stranger on the beach.

We can't be certain as to just what occurred there on the beach or in the Upper Room or in the garden or on the Emmaus road or in the tomb; we don't know what *really* happened. Rather, we can more readily reflect on what we know *didn't* happen.

The resurrection of Jesus was not a physical resuscitation. There is certainly no indication that the disciples plotted the resuscitation of a "dead" Jesus. His risen body was somehow different from his former earthly body. Even though the scars of the crucifixion could be seen, his close friends did not recognize him at first. It's true that he ate with them and talked with them, but he also came and went in a strange fashion—through closed doors and solid walls. Before, his day-to-day bodily reactions had seemed just like theirs, but now there was a strange and frightening difference. The Apostle Paul seemed to catch a hint of the meaning of this strange difference when he wrote that "flesh and blood cannot inherit the kingdom of God, nor does the perishable inherit the imperishable" (1 Cor. 15:50, RSV).

The resurrection of Jesus was not a mental hallucination. While there is much that is missing from our understanding of the details of the death and burial of Jesus, we know that his family and his disciples were heartbroken and depressed, and that those who removed his broken body from the cross were convinced of his death. We know, too, that after the climactic event of Easter morning their gloom was dispelled and they were changed people. No longer were they frightened and cowering—now there was a boldness and a confidence about them not unlike that of Jesus. Something dramatic happened that changed the lives of those disciples —the Resurrection was a *happening,* an *event,* not a bit of beef as Scrooge defined Marley's ghost to be . . . more of gravy than the grave, not a bit of dream or fantasy or wish-projection. Its reality is demonstrated in its results— no mental hallucination here.

The resurrection of Jesus was a personal encounter of the risen Jesus in which there was communication and then ultimate recognition. Perhaps the earliest documentation of the Resurrection has been given us by Paul: "For I delivered to you as of first importance what I also received, that Christ died for our sins in accordance with the scriptures, that he was buried, that he was raised on the third day . . . that he appeared to Cephas, then to the twelve. Then he appeared to more than five hundred brethren at one time, most of whom are still alive. . . . Last of all, as to one untimely born, he appeared also to me" (1 Cor. 15:3–8, RSV).

From this we see that Paul regarded his own encounter with Christ on the Damascus road to be as valid as Christ's earlier appearances to the disciples . . . an appearance which, of course, was nonphysical.

When that stranger on the beach during those early morning hours told the fishermen to throw the net on the other side of the boat, they followed his instruction. The results were unbelievable—the nets were loaded almost to the breaking point with wiggling and flopping fish. As the weary fishermen looked on in amazement, one of them said to Peter, "It is the Lord!"

Easter Is Discernment

Easter is discernment of the risen Christ in the events of our time and in the relationships of our lives. When, like the disciples, the nets of our lives are empty and then suddenly begin to fill up with new meaning—it is the Lord! When we're preoccupied with failure or defeat, and it begins to dawn on us that nothing is final, that there's another chance, a door opening out of the wall—it is the Lord! Ernest Hemingway worded it well in an affirmation that works both ways: "Man can be defeated but not destroyed. Man can be destroyed but not defeated."

When we receive a fresh insight, when for a moment we *know* we are forgiven, when a new idea bursts from nowhere into our consciousness, when our hearts turn over and the wheels of hope start spinning again—it is the Lord! Easter is discernment of the extraordinary in the ordinary—the apprehension, as Eliot wrote, of "the point of intersection of the timeless with time."

A friend shared this thought with me during the Lenten season a few years ago: "To me, Lent is a reminder that the fullness of time precedes the pursuit of happiness. The recurring cycle of the Lenten drama is a reminder that we all get second chances in our lives—chances to catch an insight, to subdue a temperament, to hear a friend's voice, to march to a different drummer." How true. But so often the distractions bleed off our sensitivity to the Easter season. We become preoccupied with other things—right and good things—our day-to-day routines, music, art, church work, club activities, our own good times . . . and we have failed once again to participate personally and intimately in the deep meaning of Easter.

Another friend rolled aside the curtains of her deepest feelings with this moving story of insight received through what I like to think comes from a unique and

penetrating awareness of the fact of Easter. "Ten years ago
I received a scrawled, almost illegible letter from an old
lady known only to me as my California grandmother. The
letter contained this poem:

> Father Time is telling me every day
> The home I live in is wearing away.
> The building is old and for the days that remain,
> To seek to repair it would be quite in vain.
> So I'm getting ready to move."

My friend continued, "One day soon afterwards
I discovered that my grandmother had moved when I
received all the letters and photos I had sent her over the
years. They were carefully arranged in a red leather case
with handwritten instructions on the outside to send the
contents to me. That afternoon I sat down to go through
the many pieces which were in the package: birthday
greetings sketched in the erratic hand of a five-year-old;
crayoned hearts for Valentine's Day; my first school
picture; long letters of a thirteen-year-old which poured
out feelings and problems too private for anyone closer to
home. As I looked at my life through her eyes, it was an
eerie, solemn moment. Beyond the sadness of her death and
the nostalgia of my own memories, I suddenly realized that
in preparation for her leave-taking my grandmother had
arranged to send her part of my life back to me; she was
giving back to me all that she loved about me—only better
because she was now part of it. As I sit now pondering
these things, I realize anew how she had left me alone to
give witness to what we had once shared together. I am a
witness for her, for myself, for our friendship. And I know
that in some inexplicable way, marked by the deepest sadness,
the greatest joy, and a bundle of old letters, I have been
made a new person through the gift I received from her."
Easter is the time to celebrate our discernments,

to remember those times when we cried out of the deepest
sadness or the greatest joy, "It is the Lord!"

Several years ago I attended a seminar on
creativity with a group of friends. It was a fascinating time
of exploring our own individual creativity, how it is stifled
and released. In the worship service on the last day people
shared the insights that had come to them during the weekend.
One woman shared a simple but significant discovery.
Though she didn't say so, I think she had been suffering
from an overdose of the "feminist mystique"—that is, the
feeling that every woman must have a "career" and spend
at least five nights a week at meetings and be twice as smart
as her husband. But as a result of our time together she
said with great relief and gratitude, "In these days I've come
to realize that my vocation now is to be a wife and mother."
Then she hesitated, looked at her husband, and said, "No,
John's wife."

It was a beautiful affirmation of her husband,
their marriage, her own vocation. And it was a recognition
of the fact that there is no art so demanding of creativity
and imagination as the *art of loving* a child, a husband or
wife, friend, colleague, parent. It seems to me that we talk
a lot about brotherhood, as we must and should, but I also
believe we should talk more about friendhood, wifehood,
and husbandhood.

Years ago I came home late for dinner one
evening after being engaged all afternoon calling on members
of my congregation. I was met at the door by my wife, hair
standing on end, a screaming baby in one arm, and a soiled
diaper on the other. Her first words were, "Why don't you
call on me sometime?" You could say it was a discernment
situation for me. I don't recall saying, "It is the Lord," but
at that moment I understood exactly how she must feel.
Unfortunately, I never seem to learn, but need to be
constantly reminded that I have neglected or have been
insensitive to the people who are closest to me in my family

and at work. It seems that we can be so involved earning money, getting ahead, doing our duty, keeping the house spotless, or saving the world while our own personal relationships disintegrate.

A friend of mine showed me a letter from his son, a college sophomore, which began, "Beloved Father." The letter was made up entirely of a marvelous, witty, and affectionate journey through his current thoughts, escapades, and hopes. As I read the letter, I reflected on how this father must have done a lot of right things to have a son who felt free to share his life in such a natural way. And then I thought of sons and daughters who seldom write their parents, and when they do, the letters are nothing more than perfunctory notes. What a tragedy it is, for whatever reason, when sons and daughters are unable to share their lives with their parents!

What a liberating experience it is at the Easter season to be able to celebrate our discernments as we remember those times when we have cried out of the deepest sadness or the greatest joy, "It is the Lord!"

Easter Is Commitment

Easter is commitment to feed the Lord's sheep—the Lord's people—all of his sheep, the black sheep, the sheep in wolves' clothing . . . every last, lost, and least one of his human flock. Discernment of the risen Lord is authenticated by our commitment to feed his hungry sheep—to serve and relate to his people. All around us are lonely and alienated people who are looking at us and asking, "Do you love me?" even as Jesus did three times of Peter. Then you will recall that Peter answered, "Lord, you know I love you," and Jesus responded, "Feed my sheep."

In his play *A Delicate Balance* Edward Albee probes the rights and responsibilities of friendship. On a Friday night—Good Friday—Harry and Edna go to the

home of their dearest friends, Tobias and Agnes. Harry
and Edna have had a strange and terrifying experience of
emptiness, of dreadful lostness such as comes to children in
the dark. In desperation they have come to the home of their
friends . . . to stay . . . to move in . . . to live with them.

After Agnes has taken them to the guest room,
she tells Tobias that their friends are ill—victims of a deadly
plague—that neither of them is immune, and that it is quite
possible the delicate balance of their family life may be
destroyed.

Tobias replies, "What am I supposed to do?
Say: 'Look, you can't stay here, you've got trouble. You are
friends, but you've got to be clean to stay here.' Well, I can't
do that. No, Agnes, if that's all Harry and Edna mean to us,
then what about us? When *we* touch; when *we* promise;
when *we* say yes, but only *if* . . . if there's any condition,
Agnes, then it's all been empty."

Saturday Harry and Edna stay right in their
room. Throughout the day and late into the night Tobias
agonizes over his questions. What are the limits of friendship?
. . . Would you borrow money for a friend? . . . Would you
lay down your life for a friend?

Early on Sunday morning—Easterday—Harry
and Edna emerge from the seclusion of their room and
come downstairs. They have decided to go back home, but
Tobias has worked through his struggle and urges them to
stay.

"Do you want us here, Tobias?" Harry asks.

Tobias begins to lose control of his emotions,
and on the edge of hysteria, he shouts, "Of course I want you
here. I built this house and you are welcome here even
though you've got this plague. You're our friends, our very
best friends in the world, and you don't have to ask. We
love each other, don't we? Doesn't friendship grow to
that . . . to love? Doesn't forty years amount to
anything?" . . .

In this remarkable play Albee probes our
friendships, our loves, our ethics, and tells us that unless we
act out our love for family and friends, our love is empty
and phony.

Who are *our* friends? Who are those imposing
on us, calling to us, "Do you love me?" I believe they are the
voices and the faces of our friends . . . and those other "sheep."

There are the voice and face of a poor little
rich girl who lives in a big house where there is little love . . .
the poor little rich girl who cries, "Do you love me?"

There are the voices and faces of the poor . . .
the hopeless man who is hard-core unemployable . . . the
gaunt face of a child in India who is marked for death by
malnutrition . . . the multicolored faces of all the have-nots
of the world looking to us—the haves—with the eyes of Jesus,
and asking, "Do you love me?"

There are the voice and face of the old woman
in a hospital, so graciously silent and patient, so alone and
unwanted and unneeded—so forgotten. And her silent eyes
are asking, "Do you love me?"

Easter is commitment—the commitment to feed
the Lord's sheep, to reach out with feeling love and action to
people everywhere. The power of the Resurrection is to see
Jesus, to know him, and to care deeply. May it not be said
of me that Jesus stood on the beach and I didn't know it
was he.

New Life from Dry Bones

Maurice M. Benitez

The hand of the Lord was upon me, and he brought me out by the Spirit of the Lord, and set me down in the midst of the valley; it was full of bones. And he led me round among them; and behold, there were very many upon the valley; and lo, they were very dry. And he said to me, "Son of Man, can these bones live?" And I answered, "O Lord God, thou knowest." Again he said to me, "Prophesy to these bones, and say to them, O dry bones, hear the word of the Lord." Thus says the Lord God to these bones: Behold, I will cause breath to enter you, and you shall live.

(Ezekiel 37:1–5, RSV)

In a time of death, desolation, smashed hopes, bitter defeat, and emotional and physical slavery, God spoke through the prophet Ezekiel, "I will cause breath to enter you, and you shall live."

Here in dramatic fashion God broke into human history through the vision of Ezekiel when the Lord set him down in the middle of an accumulation of dry bones—lifeless, useless, seemingly forgotten, but not forgotten by God. Israel, God's special people—the dry bones—were in exile far from home. Their defeat by the Babylonian army had been complete and their humiliation had plunged them into a deadly and soul-bleaching despair. But into this desolate scene stepped the prophet of God with a message of hope: "You shall live."

And we have a strong hint in this strange story of a moment some five hundred years later when on that first Easter morning the blackness of death dissolved into the sunrise of new life, when Jesus in resurrection glory stepped out of Joseph's tomb. Out of the defeat of an excruciating death on Good Friday came resurrection victory . . . out of despair came a living hope . . . out of what seemed to be the end, Jesus brought a new beginning. Out of dry bones came a new body—a signal for all time of new hope, of new life.

But those were baffling and fearful moments for the disciples and friends of Jesus on that first Easter morning, and for days after. Jesus appeared first to his most intimate friends, Peter and John. And then he showed himself to a small group of women who had slipped out to the tomb in the early morning hours with spices to anoint his body.

Next he appeared to the rest of his disciples. They were all amazed and shocked. It was incomprehensible; dead people stay dead, but Jesus was alive! On Friday he was dead and buried, and now he was alive again.

Over the next forty days Jesus appeared to friends on several different occasions. He ate with them, walked and talked with them. They were convinced he was alive. Their witness was not just that the grave was empty—rather, it was that Christ was alive. This Jesus who was crucified, God had raised from the dead! He is the Son of God, and the future is in his hands.

This mind-boggling fact revolutionized their pattern of life. No longer were they a confused cadre of people clustered fearfully around a dead cause. Rather, they were a transformed and electrified group of witnesses with a dynamic message about a risen Christ which literally exploded across the countryside. Life-changing miracles became commonplace wherever people heard the startling good news—and there began then a life-changing chain reaction which has reverberated across the intervening years into both our present and our future. In the fulfillment of Ezekiel's prophecy, God gives new life through Jesus Christ . . . a new living Spirit to our dead bones.

And it is through this awesome event—all that led up to it, and all which follows—that we in these closing years of the twentieth century and especially in the 1980s can find a living and lasting and workable hope.

First, *there is hope for us as people.* In the Apostle Paul's words, we can do *all* things through Christ who strengthens us. If God can give new life to dry bones, he can breathe new life into each of us and infuse us with the energy of the Holy Spirit so that our deepest hurts are healed and our profoundest needs are met in the raw give-and-take of life right now. And if God could breathe new life into Jesus and propel him from the tomb on that first Easter morning, there is no mistake we can make nor sin we can commit that will move us outside the redemptive grace unleashed at the moment of Resurrection.

And then *the Easter message of hope is for this world.* We today live in a bewildered society. We listen to radio and television news and ponder the complexities of peace and war in the Middle East and in the Third World. Countries and people who were once friends are now name-calling enemies. Treachery and self-service seem to motivate so much that goes on, and through energy and gasoline shortages and high prices we feel the hostility and greed of many former friends. We find ourselves in a shrunken and troubled world—traumatized by the fear of nuclear accidents, crippling inflation, political uncertainties, crime at home, and hunger abroad. There is fear all about us, and the smell of death is in the air.

But Easter and the events leading up to it remind us that God is still in control. This is his world, and he has the last word. History is rich in moments when it seemed there was no hope, there were no solutions. But what seemed like the end was really the new beginning—the Cross cast a frightening shadow of doom across the frantic efforts of people everywhere, yet Resurrection brought life and hope.

If God can give new life to dead bones and raise Jesus from a tomb, he can, today, breathe new life into our troubled world. But he works through the dedicated efforts of his people wherever they are found. By God's grace, you and I have the potential to change the world. We can demonstrate a way of wholeness that gives our day-to-day life new meaning. We can proclaim our Easter message and work to make this world the kind of place that God would have it be, with the radiant hope that, come what may, we are forever and wonderfully in the hands of God.

And then *the Easter message promises that physical death is not the end*—God will give new flesh to our dry bones in life beyond the grave. The lessons learned, the maturity gained here and now is not lost in oblivion—rather our training here as Christians will serve us well in God's future economy. The writer of the Book of Hebrews laid it out pretty well and hinted strongly at the promise of the future when he wrote, "Therefore, since we are surrounded by so great a cloud of witnesses, let us also lay aside every weight, and sin which clings so closely, and let us run with perseverance the race that is set before us" (Heb. 12:1, RSV).

I've always been inspired as I reflect on a story told by Lou Little, who for many years was the football coach at Columbia University. He had a young, third-string quarterback who was in his senior year. The young man was small and had little natural ability, yet for three years he had given the best he had in practice throughout the week even though he never played a minute on Saturday afternoon.

Toward the close of the season the young quarterback mysteriously missed practice on both Thursday and Friday before an important game—something most unusual for him. But he showed up before game time on Saturday, and with a strange look on his face, he pleaded, "Coach, I've never asked anything like this before, but please let me start the game today. Please. . . ."

Lou Little was reluctant, but there was a compelling urgency about the boy that was somehow irresistible. Besides, this hadn't been a good season, and it was predicted they would lose the game by a wide margin. There seemed little to lose so he put the young man in the starting lineup. He was sensational from the opening play on. Instead of pulling the boy out after a few minutes of play as he had planned, Little left him in for the entire game. He played an inspired game and through his leadership and the superhuman efforts of his teammates, they pulled off the upset of the year and won by a wide margin.

After the game, with tears glistening in his eyes

but with a radiant look on his face, the young quarterback explained, "Coach, my dad was blinded when I was a small boy. He never saw me play football. He died earlier this week, and that's why I missed practice on Thursday and Friday. But today, I knew that for the first time he could see me play—that's why I just had to get in that game."

Finally, for me, the greatest miracle of Easter is not just that Jesus rose from the dead, but that we can be risen with him now! The gift of God to us is that the resurrection life of Jesus Christ can be lived out through us today and tomorrow. He is alive in us right now! ". . . it is no longer I who live, but Christ who lives in me . . ." (Gal. 2:20, RSV). Eternal life for the Christian does not begin at death—it is ours here and now in the hurly-burly of life as we live it out with our loved ones and friends and business relationships twenty-four hours at a time.

One day someone asked me, "Why was Jesus crucified? Why the cross?"

Almost without thinking I responded, "I guess that's what it took to get me into Christ's kingdom." And I have come now to believe my impulsive answer was the wisdom of the ages.

Today if someone were to ask, "Why the Resurrection? Why was Jesus raised from the dead?" I'd reply, "I guess that's what it took to give new life to my dry bones." And my Easter message to the world and to each one of you is that if you will let him, God will give that same glorious new life to your dry bones!

Easter as a Hope

James I. McCord

Therefore, my beloved brethren, be
steadfast, immovable, always abounding
in the work of the Lord, knowing that in
the Lord your labor is not in vain.

(1 Corinthians 15:58, RSV)

After an arid and somewhat arrogant period during which we were deluded by the notion that the present is the capstone of creation, there has crept into our consciousness the growing awareness of a tug from the past. How sad it is that our nostalgia itch failed to emerge before so many symbols of our heritage suffered an ignoble fate from the bulldozer's blade under the excuse of progress. Now asphalt, concrete, and steel reflect an awesome sterility quite symbolic of the thinness of our times and the slippage in our values.

And yet possibly the pendulum is swinging. In 1976 American people everywhere paid lip service at least in some degree to the 200th anniversary of the founding of the United States of America. This awareness was further sharpened by the popularity of *Roots*, both as a book and as a television special.

Still we find it incredibly difficult to focus long on the past because we are haunted by the specter of the next few years. So much of what has mattered to us—low-cost energy, an abundant supply of gasoline and fuel, a relatively stable economy since the late 1930s and early 1940s—is slipping away, creating a puzzling unsureness and insecurity. However, we are not only knotted up by the usual fears of the unknown, the passing of the old and familiar and the strangeness of the new and disturbing, but for those millions born during and since World War II there is an added dimension of dread—the possibility of no future at all. This generation especially was born under and has lived with the threat of atomic and nuclear extinction. With childhood came dire predictions of overpopulation and mass starvation, predictions that are now being fulfilled in many parts of the world. With maturity came the rumblings of the ecological crisis, an abrupt awareness of the wanton abuse of creation, of a seeming breakdown and disintegration of our planet, with dying and dead oceans and streams, and with an atmosphere polluted and choked by man-made waste. And more recently, the threat of genetic control and a host of other biological menaces have wreaked havoc in our already soaring anxiety levels.

So bleak has been the verdict that multiplied millions feel doomed to live in a world without hope and shorn of a future. Certainly, in large measure this accounts for our striving for instant gratification and dilutes our capability to take the long view. As members of the "instant" generation, we feel robbed of time, abandoned to the present, and delivered over to the futurologists. And these scientists, or pseudoscientists, seem to be the new prophets of doom whose stock in trade are predictions of imminent catastrophe.

Against this background the Easter message is heard today. It is the proclamation of hope in spite of all evidence to the contrary, and hope has been defined as "patience with the lamp lit." Easter means that in spite of human failure and sin God has taken up our cause as *his* cause, and in Jesus Christ has made our future his future.

In the New Testament the Resurrection and Ascension are seen from two perspectives. They are two sides of a single event: the raising of Jesus from the dead and his enthronement on the right hand of God. From another perspective these two sides are pulled apart for a period of forty days, and we are allowed to see the risen Christ discussing with his disciples "the things pertaining to the kingdom of God." The scenes depicted during this time are among the most majestic in the entire Bible. Christ, having triumphed over death and standing on this side of the Easter morning event, claims all power in heaven and on earth for

himself. He is about to be installed in complete authority
and power, and during these days Jesus is equipping the
disciples for his continuing ministry in the world. But it is
just at this point that they ask him for a lesson in futurology:
"Lord, wilt thou at this time restore again the kingdom to
Israel?" His response is blunt: "It is not for you to know the
[general] times or the [specific] seasons, which the Father
hath put in his own power. But you shall receive power,
after that the Holy Ghost is come upon you: and you shall
be witnesses of me . . ." (Acts 1:6–8, KJV).

In this dialogue between Christ and his disciples,
cryptic as it is, there is a profound message for us as we
contemplate these closing years of the twentieth century.

For one thing, while the futurologist of today
performs a valuable service through warning us of our abuse
of creation and its devastating consequences, he claims to
know *too* much. It was the Yugoslav Djilas who said that
"the future is known only to gods and dogmatists." Those
who try to unravel the future as if they have some private
knowledge of dates on the celestial calendar have always
been embarrassed by the failure of their predictions. It was
true in the early history of the church when the followers
of Montanus assembled together in Asia Minor to await an
end that did not come. Later on it was true of the gloomy
preacher, Thomas Malthus, with his picture of society snared
in a hopeless trap sprung of population's growth outstripping
all possible means of support. And it is equally true today
of those who attempt to set the date for the demise of
planet Earth.

Biblically speaking, the end is not a date on a
calendar. Rather, it is related to our obedience. Our Lord
said, "And this gospel of the kingdom shall be preached in
all the world for a witness unto all nations; and then shall the
end come" (Matt. 24:14, KJV). And for the Christian the
end means fulfillment, the completion of God's plan.

Today's futurologist, while claiming to know so

much about tomorrow, fails to understand either the nature of God or of the human enterprise. The God of the Bible is no mere spectator, aloof and apart, content to witness human foolishness and merely await the destruction of his creation. He has never abdicated authority over the world, nor has he relinquished control. Rather, he continues to be vitally interested in human affairs and intimately involved in human history.

This is basic to our faith today. God is the God of the promises, the God of the future. When Moses was commissioned to lead Israel out of slavery and asked God to reveal his character by giving his name, God answered, "I will be what I will be"; I will be tomorrow what I am today; I *am* the God on whom my people can depend.

The God of the promises is also the God and Father of our Lord Jesus Christ. It was to him that Jesus committed his spirit as he surrendered to the bondage of death on the cross in full confidence that his future could be trusted to God.

This same faith was found in many of those who first settled on our eastern shores and laid the sturdy foundation of the American republic. They were animated by a strong faith in God and a deep sense of vocation. These intrepid early settlers who carved a new civilization from the wilderness believed that God was at work in the world and had called them to be partners in his enterprise. They were acutely conscious of taking part in an exodus from an old world with its stifling, outmoded, and unjust structures to a new world where a "Zion in the wilderness" would be built. Here was a pilgrim people, convinced that this was a part of divine providence with which they were cooperating. The diary of John Quincy Adams, a superb legacy from those early days, makes clear that the driving force behind his struggle with a nation on what he believed to be a moral principle was his firm belief that God was in control and that God's will would ultimately prevail. Our ancestors did not back into the future; they entered it with courage in the company of the living God.

And then, today's futurologist, like his predecessors throughout the history of the Christian Church, is producing paralysis in society. While he hopes through his warnings to persuade us to change our ways, the result is too often in the opposite direction. But this is nothing new. When the first one thousand years of Christian history ended, many thought the end of the world was at hand. They neglected to plant crops and waited for the curtain to fall. The results were catastrophic.

But today's paralysis is of a different character. We have become excessively absorbed with ourselves and are involved in an endless analysis of our personal and cultural neuroses. We are told that we are involved in situations that are so radically different from anything in the past that history has nothing to teach us. We are ignoring Santayana's dictum that "those who forget the past are condemned to repeat it." Our preoccupation with questionnaires, continually gathering data about the present, has succeeded in turning us into the most analyzed generation in history. There is very little, if anything, that has not been measured or counted.

While we are the most analyzed generation, we have become the generation least able to cope. We have abandoned matters of primary importance, no longer asking what is right or wrong but how does it make us feel.

It seems to me, too, that today's futurologist has, tragically, missed the most important lesson of all—the redemptive element in history. And the authentic meaning of history is justification by faith and forgiveness of sin.

This eternal truth is not only valid in history, it is infinitely true in our own lives as persons. Being a Christian means that our past with all its burdens is canceled when our sins are forgiven, and that God opens up a new future filled with fresh possibilities for us when he justifies us by faith. Then we know firsthand the experience of being freed through God's redeeming grace. And it happens to us again and again when we confess and are forgiven.

Happily, this same redemptive possibility prevails throughout all human existence and God's creation. He is able to overcome our senseless mistakes and to create new opportunities for building a world that is just and humane—one free from the genocide in certain parts of the world today, one in which hopeless refugees from the indescribable horrors of war are welcomed with compassion and understanding . . . a world more in accord with God's intention for his people and fit for human habitation.

Easter is the guarantee of all this. It has meaning for persons and nations. The Easter event began when the Word became flesh, when God and man were united forever in Jesus Christ. In this supreme act of love God took our future upon himself, and at Easter life triumphed over death for all time.

I would like to see the celebration of Easter begin at midnight as it was observed by Orthodox Christians in precommunist Russia. In St. Petersburg, for example, the Cathedral of St. Isaac was jammed with the faithful as they waited in total darkness for the stroke of midnight. Then as the hour struck, the guns from the fortress of St. Peter and St. Paul boomed their salute of the new day, the huge doors of the majestic cathedral were thrown open, candles were lit, and the choir entered and moved down the aisle singing the triumphant Easter anthem. This was a moment of intense emotion, of historic drama.

Such is the drama of Easter. It is that overwhelming awareness of the presence of God coursing through our day-to-day struggles to maintain a home, raise children, earn a living, and get along reasonably well with family and neighbors. It represents the triumph of light over darkness, freedom from emotional and physical bondage . . . hope over alienation and despair . . . life over death. It is the miracle of God's grace that enables us to rise above the perils of today and to become witnesses and partners in his work of making *all* things new.

One of the most moving and majestic passages of all literature was written by the Apostle Paul to Corinthian Christians. In 1 Corinthians 15 the Apostle's all-inclusive statement of the Resurrection is found. Here in unequaled prose Paul acknowledges the *fact* of the Resurrection . . . he presents unquestionable *assurance* of the Resurrection . . . he argues eloquently the *logic* of the Resurrection . . . he carefully explains the *nature* of the Resurrection . . . and he boldly announces the *triumph* of the Resurrection.

Then Paul completes his dramatic statement with, "But thanks be to God, who giveth us the victory through our Lord Jesus Christ." But he doesn't stop there, for as a result of the Resurrection of Christ on that first Easter morning, we are liberated to serve the living God. And so he concludes with this call to action: "Therefore, my beloved brethren, be steadfast, immovable, always abounding in the work of the Lord, knowing that in the Lord your labor is not in vain."

Easter is not a passive reaction to a historic event. Instead, it demands a positive response, translated into action . . . it galvanizes hope for today and tomorrow. Easter is hope!

The Easter People

Alan Walker

Now Thomas, one of the twelve, called the Twin, was not with them when Jesus came. So the other disciples told him, "We have seen the Lord."

(John 20:24–25, RSV)

On a certain Friday a group of people saw the leader to whom they had committed their lives crucified on a cross. Bewildered, heartbroken, they had watched him die, and late that afternoon saw his dead body placed in a tomb. When the heavy stone thudded across the door of the tomb and was secured by the seal of the Roman Empire, it also crashed through the corridors of their minds, demolishing forever all their hopes and dreams. In black despair, blind confusion, and shattering disillusionment they scattered furtively across the country, determined to resume the vocations they had left abruptly over three years before.

Within a few weeks all of this was changed. The scattered followers of Jesus came together again, filled with confidence, joy, and purpose. In the very city where Jesus had been publicly executed they launched the most powerful and dynamic crusade in history. Something obviously had happened!

The cross of defeat suddenly became the symbol of victory. The message became not what Jesus of Nazareth taught, but the person of Jesus himself. And the Christian Church began its unpredictable course through history.

Something obviously happened! What was it?

The event of Easter day provides the answer. The followers and friends of Jesus believed without question that while he had died on Friday afternoon, he was now alive.

How did they know? It certainly wasn't because any of them had seen Jesus burst through the stone door in a blaze of glory. It was not because his body had disappeared. True, it had vanished, but there could be several logical explanations for that. And, it was not simply because the tomb was empty, for, after all, there's no power in a vacuum.

These people knew that Jesus was alive because they saw him and talked with him. For almost six weeks Jesus appeared to a person here, two disciples there, to a group, a crowd. He was seen in several different locations—in a room, in the open, along a country road, by the Sea of Galilee. At least as far as the written record is concerned, he was always seen during the day, never at night. And every encounter radiated a tremendous self-authenticating power.

Now, as then, the miracle of Easter is discovered through personal encounters with the living Christ. This is what makes the difference. And this is what produces Easter people. It is all built on the simple testimony recorded in John 20:25, "We have seen the Lord."

A New Belief

It was from those early encounters with the risen Christ that a new belief emerged—the historic faith which soon became known as Christianity.

And the foundation for that faith is that "God raised Jesus from the dead," even though the resurrection of Jesus was neither expected nor inevitable. Certainly Jesus had no more power within himself to raise his own body from the dead than any other man. The miracle of Easter is God's miracle; "God raised Jesus from the dead."

A Christian believes that God, by raising Jesus from the dead, accepted, endorsed, verified everything he was and did. God by this mighty act showed where he stood. He took the side of Jesus, declaring his truth was abiding, while the attitude and actions of his enemies were wrong.

Now we can be sure Jesus was God's revealer. The words of Jesus are the words of God. The acts of Jesus are the acts of God. The suffering of Jesus reflects the suffering of God, and the victory of Jesus became the victory of God.

From the vindication of Jesus comes his abiding authority. In the first century Christians declared a simple creed: "Jesus Christ is Lord." It became the truth for which men and women both lived and died. The words and actions of Jesus became for his followers the representation of eternal authority.

Slowly over the years, the Christian interpretation of the universe, of life, of history was fashioned. Led especially by the gigantic mind of the Apostle Paul, the structure we call Christian doctrine emerged. Logically, powerfully, it became the most comprehensive and satisfying interpretation of life, and it continues to have this wholeness of understanding. Yet it is all built on one mighty act of God: "God raised Jesus Christ from the dead." And that conviction in turn rested on the claim of the early disciples: "We have seen the Lord." It led to a new belief.

A New Community

Out of the encounter with the risen Christ came a new community called the Church.

With amazing speed a new community with its own belief, its own life style, its own fellowship, its own purpose came into being. So distinctive was it that it quickly became identifiable. It was given a new name: the Way. The primitive title given to Christians appears six times in the Acts of the Apostles. The followers of Jesus were called People of the Way.

Dr. Lesslie Newbigin says: "Jesus left behind him not a book, nor a creed, nor a system of thought, nor a rule of life, but a visible community."

But what a community the Church proved to be! For three hundred years it existed without owning any property, having no visible presence except in the lives of

Christians, yet it spread like a forest fire across the world of that day. Since that time it has survived vast social and historic changes. It has outlived empires, and it has persisted through upheavals like the Renaissance, the birth of the Industrial Revolution, the French and the Communist revolutions.

Today the new community called the Church is a global reality. It has become the only universal faith of history. And still it grows. In Asia, Latin America, the Pacific, and Africa it is advancing at unprecedented speed.

For example, in 1875 there were 500,000 Christians on the African continent. By 1925 the church numbered 5,000,000 people. By 1975 there were 100,000,000 Christians in Africa, and it is believed by some Christian leaders that by the year 2000 the strength of Christianity will be centered in Africa.

How can a miracle of this magnitude be explained? Only by seeing the risen Christ at its heart; the energy of the Resurrection which brought Jesus from the dead continues to throb through the Church.

The risen Christ created a new community, the Church.

A New Cause

Out of the encounter with the living Christ came a new cause: the kingdom of God on earth.

The Catholic theologian Dr. Hans Küng claims: "For the apostles and St. Paul appearance and vocation, encounter and mission go together." Certainly the appearances of the risen Christ before the Ascension provide the call to go forward, proclaiming the Christian message to all people. "You shall be my witnesses in Jerusalem and in all Judea and Samaria and to the end of the earth," said Jesus (Acts 1:8, RSV). By placing together the recorded words of Jesus in the last chapters of Mark and Matthew we hear his

double Commission: "Go into all the world and preach
the gospel to the whole creation . . . and make disciples of
all nations. . . ."

The Christian task is an unfinished task. Because
of the population explosion there are in the world today
more people who know little or nothing about Jesus Christ
than ever before in history. Therefore the risen Christ
commands obedience in mission as always. He points to a
world yet to become the kingdom of God.

The risen Christ directs every person who
accepts his authority to the social and international evils of
our time. He lifts to consciousness the dread trio of world
problems: poverty, racism, and war. He points us toward
the goal of working for an economic system of far greater
equality and justice than we know today, and he bids us
struggle on until the last vestiges of racism are swept away.
And as the greatest exponent of nonviolence in history,
Jesus engages us in the task finally to banish war from the
human scene.

A New Future

Out of the experience of the risen Christ comes
a new future.

The happenings of the first Good Friday, the
crucifixion of Jesus, meant that the early disciples had a past
but no future. It seemed that Jesus had finished his story.

There is a terrible finality about death. At the
moment of death everything seems frozen. No more words
can be spoken, no new acts can be performed, and no
further relationships can be established. There is only
yesterday—no tomorrow. All that little cadre of disciples
could do was to say brokenly: "We had hoped he was the
One to redeem Israel." We had hoped! Now it was all
over. Death is so final.

But suddenly, with the resurrection of Jesus,

there *was* a future. Hope was born anew. "Go tell my disciples, and Peter, I shall meet them in Galilee." New words were spoken, new and strange events shook the credulity of his friends, and a new love, the love of the risen Christ, flooded the hearts of his followers.

That future—what was started then—has never ended. We're still on the receiving end of new revelations, new directions, new power from the risen Christ to handle the complexities of life in these last and fast-moving years of the twentieth century. Today his living mind and heart direct the life of the church, and we can commune with Jesus as friend with friend—the only difference being that we cannot see him with our physical eyes.

The risen Christ gives us a future when we are battered by sin and despair and feelings of alienation. John Wesley said once: "It takes as great a miracle to bring a man or woman from the sepulchre of sin as to bring Christ's body from the tomb." By the ever-present grace of God that miracle occurs day after day in the lives of people as they discover new meaning and wholeness in the Good News through commitment to Jesus Christ as Lord.

Let me tell you the story of an Australian girl named Vicki. At sixteen years of age she attended church regularly and sang in the choir. But it wasn't long before she got mixed up with a group of friends who were experimenting with alcohol and drugs. She gave every appearance of being "stoned" much of the time—eyes glazed, voice thick, skin discolored. In spite of the concern of her many friends Vicki continued on her tragic way. We knew that if something dramatic didn't happen Vicki could well be dead by the time she was twenty-five years of age.

Recently she stood before the television cameras in a worship service televised from Sydney, Australia, and quietly told her story. "I knew the Christian message, but for years I rejected Christ. Then one day in desperation I said, 'God, why don't you come close to me?' He replied,

'Vicki, I cannot come any closer to you, I am with you now.'
Suddenly I was overcome with the thought of his infinite
patience. Even though I had rejected him a hundred times
yet he was with me still. And at that moment I accepted
Jesus Christ. Look, I am free." And she was. Now her eyes
were clear, her voice strong, her skin clear. Vicki now had
a future.

At the heart of the Easter message is an encounter
with the living Christ. And it is this encounter which daily,
as our lives are open to him, gives a vibrant new faith, the
richness of a new relationship, the excitement of a new
cause, and the fulfillment of a new future . . . "We have
seen the Lord."

The Mystery of Immortality and the Life Beyond

John P. Newport

If Christ has not been raised, your faith
is futile and you are still in your sins.
Then those also who have fallen asleep in
Christ have perished. If for this life only
we have hoped in Christ, we are
of all men most to be pitied. But in fact
Christ has been raised from the dead....

(1 Corinthians 15:17–20, RSV)

Why is it important to consider the mystery of immortality and the life beyond at this Easter season? Or any other time for that matter? I believe it is vitally important because all of us must face death and the end of our own lives in spite of the advances of medical science. And if we have no hope, we will lose meaning and perspective in life.

However, some people today suppress their interest in the life beyond. They feel it will make them less sensitive to the present life. In drooling over the mansions in heaven, Marx said, we neglect refugees and social justice here on earth. Others say death is too morbid or too self-centered. Dr. Elizabeth Kübler-Ross, author of *On Death and Dying*, found that most people avoid the subject. Others have been influenced by the naturalism and skepticism of our time.

But down deep, most of us want to believe in a life after death, and we want to live beyond what we know in this life. The immense publicity that the first heart transplants received witnesses indirectly to our desire to prolong our lives and to escape from death. And we also want to believe that our loved ones live on beyond death.

In reflecting on these rather startling truths we are not thinking primarily about subpersonal or less than personal views of immortality. Of course, we all want to live on in our children. Tennessee Williams has one of his characters in *Baby Doll* demand that his daughter get married and furnish him with what he called "seed" (biological immortality). And there are those who seem to claim immortality through the influence of gifts, charities, books, good deeds, and living in the memories of friends

(social immortality). The Hindus talk of being absorbed up
in a higher self or Brahman (impersonal immortality).
Modern process theologians often talk of being remembered
in the mind of God (subjective immortality). But we are
primarily concerned with objective personal immortality.

The great philosophers and thinkers have
offered many arguments for immortality.

1. Buried deeply within each of us is the desire
to believe in immortality (historical argument). Like a homing
pigeon, people want to make their way to God and fulfillment
beyond death.

2. Life as we know it seems so incomplete
(teleological argument). Victor Hugo, at age seventy, wrote:
"Winter is on my head, but Spring is in my heart. I have not
said one-thousandth part of what is in me."

3. For others, life is irrational if there is no
hereafter (rational argument). G. H. Palmer, as he looked
at the body of his dead wife, killed in an auto accident,
said, "This world is irrational if, because of a driver's careless
turn, so fair a spirit is excluded forever from the universe."

4. Still others believe that there is no justice in
the world if wicked and sinful people are not held in being
for punishment beyond death (ethical argument).

5. And some people continue to affirm that
through extrasensory perception and even in resuscitation
experiences it is proven that people live beyond the grave
(psychic argument).

All of these arguments may have some appeal.
However, if we look at humankind in a more realistic and
comprehensive way, I believe that viewpoints concerning the
life hereafter can really be grouped under three models or
approaches.

First, there is what is called the nonsentimental
(naturalistic) approach. I call it the "when you are dead,
you are dead" approach. This view sees life as only a
physiological process. Death is our absolute end. Our death

means no more and no less than the death of other animals. It should be accepted without any illusions.

One version of this view makes much of the idea that personality is totally brain-dependent. We survive only when our brain cells are alive. Artificial parts can replace other decaying segments of the body, but once our brain cells die, the self dies. (I might add that the mind-body relationship is one of the oldest problems related to human personality. Schizophrenia and other mental aberrations continue to upset simple solutions.)

A second approach is called natural or innate immortality, or the idealist model. I call it the "make-it-under-your-own-steam" approach. This is the view of Plato, the Hindus and the spiritualists. Maybe one-half of all the people in the world today hold a form of this approach.

From earliest times, people have thought too highly of themselves to accept the naturalistic view of death as final. Primitive man believed that in his body dwelt a "spirit" which at death departed and became a ghost.

This approach was refined by Plato in the fourth century B.C. What is true and real is the world "in" us. The soul is our divine and immortal essence. The body is its prison and is mortal. The soul shares neither the birth nor the death of the body. Its soul preexisted, and does not die when the body decays. Death is not real. Your essential self, the soul, does not die at all.

Holding this view, Socrates welcomed death as a friend. And this idealistic model has influenced much Christian thinking. When early Christian theology was being formed, this idea was widely held. In 1512–17 the view adopted by the Lateran Council of the Roman Church was greatly influenced by this Greek concept.

Closely related in many ways to the idealist view is spiritualism. For the spiritualist, the human soul is naturally immortal. You do not need God's power to live on beyond death. Most people automatically go to

Summerland. Through mediums and their helpers in
Summerland you can communicate with your loved ones.
Bishop James Pike claimed to have talked with his son, Jim,
who had committed suicide, through Arthur Ford, a medium.

Many Christians see some of the reported
communications as frauds. Other communications are seen
as examples of extrasensory perception or demonic confusion.
The Bible forbids rather than encourages attempts to
communicate with our loved ones through mediums (Deut.
18:10 ff.) or necromancers (talkers with the dead).

Closely related to spiritualism is the view of the
contemporary thanatologists (in Greek, *thanatos* means
death), such as Dr. Raymond Moody (*Life After Life*),
Dr. Kübler-Ross, and Robert Monroe (*Journeys Out of the
Body*). They have reported scores of cases of patients who
have returned from the threshold of death to report the
Other Side. They imply that, except in instances of suicide,
without any doubt there is another side, filled with happiness,
ecstasy, joy, reunion, rewards and fulfillment, peace and
bliss for everyone—seemingly without regard to one's
beliefs, spiritual state or moral practices here on earth. Their
philosophical presupposition is similar to that of the occult,
Hindu, and spiritualist views.

There are several questions which thoughtful
people ask: Were these people dead? By medical definition,
they had not died. Their fresh life is resuscitation rather than
resurrection. Dying is not the same thing as being dead. If
loss of vital signs for a brief period is followed by revival, I
do not believe they have returned from the grave.

For the Christian, the central question is: On
whose authority do we accept the reality of life after death?
The historic Christian answer is, on the authority of Jesus
Christ, of the risen Christ and those who were with him after
his resurrection for forty days. Moody's and Kübler-Ross's
works seem to show an indifference to Christ in this respect.

Jesus Christ emphasized as reported in Luke

16:19–31 that life is not peaceful and pleasant for everyone, regardless of their relationship to him. Moody and Kübler-Ross are open-ended and relativistic about the consequences of death.

The Journal of the Spiritual Counterfeits Project asserts that Satan has used thanatology books to deaden the mind against the piercing reality of death as curse and judgment. Thus Satan has effectively sealed people off from God and the gospel of Christ. Satan appears as an "angel of light" (2 Cor. 11:14). In the Bible, death is not normal and happy, but something alien and abnormal. Death is an enemy. For thanatologists death is pleasant, and there is no need for redemption and repentance before God.

The central idea of classical Hinduism is the natural immortality of the soul, including preexistence and reincarnation. The soul budded off of Brahman, or God, and fell into a body. At death, the soul automatically lives on. It goes into a temporary heaven but is almost immediately reborn. The law of Karma or automatic judgment determines the next birth according to one's conduct in a previous life.

The ultimate goal of rebirth is reunion with God, or Brahman. The soul is liberated into Nirvana or perfect rest, or complete identity with God. This view of immortality claims to explain geniuses and inequities in birth. If you are a genius, you are well on your way to final reunion with Brahman. If you are sick or deformed, you are paying for sins in a previous existence.

Those who believe in reincarnation hold that most people have little or no memory of their previous lives. They do not have the same body. The only connection is a personality similarity. And such similarity is far too common to verify any definite reincarnation. Despite some people's opinions, the Bible does not teach preexistence, natural immortality, or reincarnation.

The third approach is the biblical model of the life beyond, which is resurrection.

According to the Bible, we do not have a mortal part, the body, and an immortal part, the soul, as separate entities. We are indivisible units, a body animated by a soul. Our hope for the life beyond is based on our relationship to God and the continuing power of God.

Because of our disobedience to God, or revolt, we are separated from him, and death is related to this disobedience. It is not beautiful; it is a dreaded enemy. For the early Israelites it was a departure to the valley of shadows, or Sheol, a place of gloom.

According to the Bible, there is nothing in us that can withstand the ravages of death. We do not have a soul that is naturally or innately immortal. From a human perspective life actually comes to an end. But the good news of Christianity is that God's holiness and judgment are tempered by his mercy. He has conceived a love plan to restore our relationship to him and thus restore us to the possibility of new life here and now and eternal life hereafter.

Christ, himself sinless, endured death. Unlike Socrates, Jesus wept and trembled as he faced death. He could conquer death only by actually dying. Christ overcame the wages of sin, which is death. He can free the inner person now from the grip of sin, and later he can transform our bodies.

In Christ's resurrection, the miracle of Easter, victory has been won. Paul says, if Christ has not been raised from the dead, then those who have fallen asleep have been annihilated (1 Cor. 15:14). But now Christ has been raised and Almighty God who raised him will give life to our mortal bodies (Rom. 8:11).

Our hope is not getting rid of our bodies, but relating to God in Christ, knowing that he can transform our bodies at death or give us a resurrection body. But in a preliminary way, we can know the power of the risen Christ even now in our inner self.

Our Christian hope is more than resuscitation of

our corpses which have been buried in a cemetery. Our hope is that God will re-create or reconstitute us as individuals with appropriate spiritual bodies.

We will appear as resurrection replicas in a different world. Our new bodies will be related to these bodies on earth, but will be appropriately different. Christ's appearance on the road to Emmaus gives us some hint as to the nature of our new bodies.

Transcending all images which describe it, heaven is the final fulfillment of our personal relationship to God. To be in Christ is to be bound with close ties to our loved ones and to all of God's children.

There are enough hints in the Bible to understand that heaven is not just dull continuance. It will surely involve some memory and recognition. In fact, we will know each other more thoroughly than now. There will be no possibility of camouflage. There will surely be a new kind of growth. And since "eye hath not seen," there will be a real element of surprise.

Is such a biblical hope escapist or morbid? No! Facing the life beyond in the right way teaches us how to live. It teaches us to see life whole. George Beasley-Murray points out that biblical hope undergirds an intense present. We have a personal dynamic. This expectant attitude gives a solid sense of responsibility.

We Christians cannot embrace the Greek, Hindu, and spiritualist beliefs. We can, however, offer the world a dynamic and superior alternative from our own Christian resources.

We believe that only the Word of the living God has the resources to fill the vacuum in our national and personal lives. There is hope for us now and hereafter in Christ. It is the responsibility and privilege of each of us to appropriate and share this hope—a hope born on that first Easter morning when Jesus Christ defeated the power of death and walked out of the garden tomb.

Born to Live

David L. McKenna

. . . and I, when I am lifted up from the earth, will draw all men to myself.

(John 12:32, RSV)

Jesus had just finished being the guest of honor in the Palm Sunday parade. His archenemies, the Pharisees, had finally admitted defeat by saying, "The whole world has gone after him." There was nothing that they could do about it. For the poor and wandering teacher from Nazareth, this was his shining hour. But his highest honor was yet ahead. A short time later certain Greek visitors in Jerusalem requested a private audience with him. To be sought by the Greeks was a tribute to his popularity, not just by the poor and the outcast but by the elitists and the intellectuals of his contemporary world.

Suddenly the story takes a strange twist. When Philip told Jesus the Greek visitors wanted to talk with him, he apparently ignored the request. Rather, a mysterious shadow cast a pall over the scene and Jesus confesses the tension he feels between his *will to live* in the glory of human acceptance and acclaim and his *will to die* for the glory of God. The flavor of his tension can be felt as he says, ". . . unless a grain of wheat falls into the earth and dies, it remains alone; but if it dies, it bears much fruit."

Actually, Jesus did not appear to have difficulty in handling the acclaim of the masses who shouted "Hosanna" and waved the palm leaves during that rather amazing and somewhat boisterous parade. Even the reluctant commendation of the Pharisees didn't seem to faze him. But to be sought out by this Greek delegation certainly had to be a supreme temptation to settle back and enjoy the distinction which was now his—after the long months of striving to be heard. Recognition by these aristocrats and intellectuals of his time had to be a glamorous enticement

for this unschooled carpenter from a neighborhood and
town that was on "the wrong side of the tracks." Ambition
and human vulnerability met head on with the purpose of
God in a decisive collision. Here is where his cross began . . .
here death and life came into tension . . . here our salvation
was placed upon a pivot.

Can you imagine the massive internal tug-of-war
waging inside Jesus at this decisive moment in his life and
career? How did he respond? Instantly, one of his own
parables comes to his mind. He had used the simple and
familiar word picture of a grain of wheat many times in
his conversations and teaching. In those times, however, he
was conveying the truth to others. Now the eternal truth
revolving around the homely story is meant for Jesus himself:
". . . unless a grain of wheat falls into the earth and dies, it
remains alone; but if it dies, it bears much fruit" (John
12:24, RSV).

At this point I believe that Jesus' mind races
from the simple beauty of the parable to the very plain and
hard foundation of his preaching. A principle returns home
to haunt him and demands his decision: "He who loves his
life loses it, and he who hates his life in this world will keep
it for eternal life" (John 12:25, RSV).

There was more. A romantic idea had not only
advanced to a realistic principle, but Jesus also remembered
that he had publicly claimed the truth as the guide for his
own life and had laid down the challenge for others to follow
him: "If anyone serves me, he must follow me; and where
I am, there shall my servant be also; if anyone serves me,
the Father will honor him" (John 12:26, RSV).

Preachers and parents are the most vulnerable
people in the world. Sooner or later, they hear their bold
pronouncements come back to them as brash and
personalized truth—preachers hear it from the members
of their congregations, and parents hear it from their
children. Jesus heard his own truth echoing in his ears.

He did not back away. Instead, he found his answer in the Scriptures, always his refuge in times of temptation and crisis. This has been supremely true in my own life, especially in times of stress. This is why it is so important for us to commit the Word of God to our hearts, for there, it will remain true even if it is not immediately relevant to us. Then, in the time of temptation or crisis, the Word of the Lord will return to remind us of our prior commitment to make God our "Overwhelming First," to use C. S. Lewis's powerful words.

So often during these overwhelming moments the Word of God comes back to us through a parable we have taught, through a principle we have accepted, through a public commitment we have made, and leaves us with the very same challenge and direction for decision which we have made to others in their moments of temptation and crisis. And when we are tempted to grasp a piece of life as if it were the whole of life—whether it is public acclaim, professional reputation, affluence, personal piety, or physical existence itself—the Word of God brings us back to the truth that self must die fully if we are to live wholly for our God.

Jesus' struggle is not over yet. Truth, even when it is obvious, must be worked through our motives as well as our minds until God's Word becomes "our Word" upon which we act. Death cannot come easily for a life-affirming person like Jesus. What had been a philosophical paradox now becomes a violent confrontation between his desire to live and his willingness to die, "Now is my soul troubled. And what shall I say? 'Father, save me from this hour? . . .' " (John 12:27, RSV).

With these words, Jesus indicted once and for all an easy faith which slides through life-and-death matters with a flippant "Praise the Lord."

C. S. Lewis voiced a similar protest when he wrote: "Talk to me about the truth of religion and I'll

listen gladly. Talk to me about the duty of religion and
I'll listen submissively. But don't come talking to me about
the consolation of religion or I'll suspect that you don't
understand." [1]

Do we understand? Of course we do, especially
in today's troubled world. We may find it hard to identify
with the mind of Jesus as powerful truth is readily recalled,
but each of us feels the anguish of a troubled soul when we
must choose between our personal desires and God's holy
will.

Around our home, I am known as the one who
is constantly saying, "Let's look at the options." My pattern
of decision-making includes a listing of the "pros" and "cons"
of alternative choices. Jesus did the same thing. Hung on
the horns of a personal dilemma, he weighed the alternative
of entertaining the Greeks and basking in the glory of their
golden age. Imagine the possibility of Jesus being included
in any anthology of Greek thought along with the names of
Plato, Socrates, Pythagoras, Heraclitus, and Aristotle! Had
this been meant to be, many people down through the ages
would have been inspired and some might even have been
changed by his teaching. But there was another option—to
drink fully from the bittersweet cup of death which seemed
to offer only the dregs of social disgrace, bodily pain, and
spiritual separation. For what purpose? To do the will of
God and fulfill the purpose for which Jesus had come.
Jesus was convinced that he was *born to die*, but he had no
certainty that he was *born to live*. So, when the issue was
finally drawn, he chose neither death nor life. He chose
God: ". . . for this purpose I have come to this hour. Father,
glorify thy name . . ." (John 12:27–28, RSV).

How did God respond to Jesus' reckless act of
faith? "Then a voice came from heaven, 'I have glorified it,
and I will glorify it again'" (John 12:28, RSV).

---

[1] C. S. Lewis, *A Grief Observed* (Greenwich, CT: Seabury Press, 1963),
p. 23.

Calling into remembrance all of his acts from the time of creation, through the history of the Children of Israel, and into the miracles of Jesus himself, God let his Son know that he had not lost his power to deliver those who put their trust in him.

We need a God who speaks from time to time, even today. Only on rare occasions did God break through natural forces to confirm the decisions of his Son. It happened once when Jesus was baptized by John and once when Jesus stood on the Mountain of Transfiguration with Moses and Elijah. Now, when Jesus chooses to do the will of God rather than accept the glory of the Greeks, God speaks again. Why? Jesus tells the crowd, "This voice has come for your sake, not for mine."

No longer did the Sonship of Jesus need to be confirmed. But he, with us, needed the confirmation of God for a life-and-death decision at the point where he was most vulnerable. A day or so later Jesus would have to kneel alone in the Garden of Gethsemane as he struggled with the coming agony of physical death. No voice from heaven was heard then; no angels ministered to him. And then a day later when Jesus was on the cross, God not only remained silent, but severed even spiritual supports so that Jesus felt forsaken and totally alone.

God always responds to us at the level of our need. When our faith is weakest and where our humanity is most vulnerable, he unfailingly comes to us with the needed confirmation. But when our faith is strong and where our humanity has been given to God, he may trust us with his silence. When matters of life and death are at stake and our faith is tested at the limits, God will come to us as we need. But the greater our faith, the more God will put us on our own, perhaps waiting three days or more to confirm our choice in the act of his new creation.

For Jesus, the weight of his decision to die tipped the scales toward life in its grandest expression short of the

Resurrection itself. First, he dealt with the false values which men hold. Jesus declared, "Now is the judgment of this world . . ." (John 12:31, rsv). All of the life-saving, death-denying values of a secular and humanistic society are forever condemned as deficient.

Next, Jesus dealt with death itself: ". . . now shall the ruler of this world be cast out" (John 12:31, rsv). *Sin*, Satan's hold on human life, is broken, and *death*, Satan's last bastion of power, is conquered.

And then Jesus begins to soar toward the affirmation of life by an acceptance of death: ". . . and I, when I am lifted up from the earth. . . ." Jesus had spoken of death before, but this was the most specific indication that he would die by crucifixion—the death with a thousand teeth. Before this time, he may not have fully absorbed this harsh truth, but now he could, not because he was nursing a sick wish for death, but because he saw the other side of the scale: "[I] will draw all men to myself."

". . . All men," not just the Greeks, but Greeks, Romans, Jews, rich and poor, whole and handicapped, black and white, male and female, east and west, north and south. Life now burst with full meaning for Jesus. Affirmative action was announced—not as a legislated form of social justice, but as the free gift of God's love for all men everywhere. Jesus knew that he was *born to live*.

Accent on Life

Arthur Fay Sueltz

If then you have been raised with Christ,
seek the things that are above, where
Christ is, seated at the right hand of God.
Set your minds on things that are above,
not on things that are on earth.

(Colossians 3:1–2, RSV)

Easter puts the accent on life. Yes, here and there a crocus blooms, and we can't stop springtime when it starts to come. But these simply point to the main theme: Life. The word *life* leads the parade of all the other words through the New Testament: "In him was life." "I am come that you might have life." "Were you not raised to life with Christ?"

I remember a young woman who in frustration went to see a marriage counselor. "My husband," she said, "has no outstanding vices. I just want to divorce him." She and the counselor talked for some time. Finally, he asked, "Don't you remember that you married him for life?"

"I know, I know," she said wearily, "but for the past five years he hasn't shown any signs of life."

Easter gives us a stark, glorious contrast between life and death, vitality and exhaustion, hope and despair. The story contains no complicated creeds or dull dogmas. All of that came later when people tried to express the inexpressible. But first of all they simply told us what they saw and heard. They sang it; they lived it; they died by it. They held onto it and it held onto them. Over and over they assured us that they saw Jesus buried in Joseph's tomb. And then on the first day of the week that very same tomb was empty, and for forty days they kept running into him. He proved his reality to them "in many infallible ways."

Peter Benchley arrived as a novelist with his book *Jaws.* In 1976 he wrote another book called *The Deep.* It's a story full of suspense about a deep-sea treasure hunt off the Bahamas. The three main characters live aboard a cabin cruiser on their first exploration after the discovery that Spanish gold lies somewhere beneath the water. Benchley describes one of the men like this: "He contemplated the possible perils and as usual found himself ambivalent toward them, nervous but excited, afraid of the unknown but impatient to meet it, eager to do things he had never done. As he looked at the dark water a shiver of anticipation made the hair on his arms rise." I'm sure this describes the feelings of Mary and Peter and John as they looked into the empty tomb Easter morning—a shiver of anticipation made the hair on their arms rise. What did it mean? Jesus had risen from the dead? This idea fit none of the categories of life as they knew it. Yet they saw the evidence with their own eyes.

But what has any of that to do with us? Even if it happened two thousand years ago, what difference does it make to us as we confront the difficult task of trying to fit the pieces of life together in our complex times?

In response to these questions the New Testament raises a question of its own, "Were *you* not raised with Christ?" (Col. 3:1). Suddenly I am faced not just with an event which occurred at a particular point in time, but I am asked a penetrating question about an experience that deeply affected human lives—a life-changing experience people continue to have today. And all at once I see a world of difference between *knowing* a fact and *experiencing* that fact as a psychological, emotional reality in my life.

I enjoy this story which Dr. Charlie Shedd tells on himself. During his early days he developed a super lecture entitled "Ten Commandments for Parents." He traveled across the country and delivered this lecture to large crowds. Then he and Martha had their first child, and shortly after he changed the lecture title to "Ten Hints for Parents." When their second child arrived, he again relabeled the lecture "A Few Tentative Suggestions for Parents." And with the arrival of their third child, he gave up the series altogether. It's one thing to know about parenthood. It is quite another thing to experience it for yourself.

Now, I need to know the facts of life. I don't want life to fool me. Especially in spiritual matters. But facts are never enough. So the New Testament talks about experience. "Were you not raised to life with Christ?" What do they mean, "raised with Christ"? I'm not dead yet. How can I be "raised with Christ"?

These are highly complex questions, but as I ponder them it dawns on me that the New Testament writer is using figurative language. And I know something about that because I use figurative language every day of my life. As Theodore Parker Ferris once suggested, if I see a person doing a hard job well, I say "he rose to the occasion." Now, when I say that, I don't literally mean that his feet left the ground. Or if I see someone wandering listlessly through life, I may say, "He looks more dead than alive," but I don't literally mean that I've seen a walking corpse. Or if I hear of someone who refuses a shady proposition, I'm likely to say, "He's above all that." And if I see someone especially happy I say, "He's on top of the world." Yet in neither of these two instances am I talking about a geographical position or location. Rather, I'm talking about something that is going on inside of a person's life. But to describe what goes on inside of a person, I'm selecting words that we customarily use to describe what is going on outside of us.

Now, I do that all the time. And so does the Bible. As I come to recognize this fact, I begin to see what this New Testament question means. It speaks figuratively about a very real inner experience. For instance, sometimes a person comes into our lives and raises us to a new level of living. For example, someone wrote of Edmund Burke, the famous writer and statesman, "If you stood in a doorway to escape a passing shower with Edmund Burke, you would leave that doorway with your shoulders back and your head up and your heart uplifted to face the realities of life."

I'm sure we've all had experiences like that with people. And I firmly believe that we cannot separate such human experiences entirely from the presence of Christ. Surely the vitality that has the power to lift human life to a new level has one source—Jesus Christ. He put new life into people everywhere he went. When he found people "down in the dumps," he lifted them up. They thought and felt badly of themselves, but Jesus raised their eyes to a new level where they could see and accept the glorious truth that they were friends and even children of God. And with the acceptance of this marvelous truth, they began to live like children of God.

Jesus often found people "down in the dumps" in their relationships with their neighbors. But with just a story he was able to raise their eyes—the story of the Good Samaritan. As I think about this scene, I discover that my neighbor isn't necessarily the one who lives closest to me, or the person who agrees with me. Rather, my neighbor is the man or woman who needs me the most.

And then all kinds of men and women around Jesus felt "down in the dumps" over failure in life. Most of them felt disgraced by failure, even as we do. But as they raised their eyes to look at Jesus, they discovered through his life that what at first might seem to be failure may in the end be simply a preview to great victory. This is true so many times with the people who move across the stage of the New Testament, and my own experience checks out with theirs. "If then we have been raised to life with Christ, aspire to the realm above. Where Christ is."

Again, using figurative language, the New Testament addresses what Viktor Frankl calls "the existential vacuum." Frankl finds at the core of human despair a profound sense that life has no meaning. No aim. No purpose.

So the New Testament now talks about the aim of life. I believe that when it talks about aspiring to the realm above where Christ is, it does not mean that I should live another worldly life. I have to live with my feet on the ground and cannot withdraw from this world with all its problems and anxieties.

I remember a friend who had a child in the fourth grade. When the child's teacher assigned them a study of the planets, she let the students choose which planet they wanted to study. So one student chose Pluto, way out there rolling around in its own way. Another student chose Mars. One little fellow chose Earth and he gave a perfectly logical reason: "I choose Earth because it's the only planet I've ever visited." So it is. And when the New Testament says, "Aspire to [or aim at] the realm above" it does not mean I should withdraw from the hassles of this world simply because I do not find them heavenly. Nor does it mean I should turn my back on great art or the achievements of technology. And it doesn't mean I should turn my back on a dollar because money is intrinsically bad. But it does mean that once Christ gets hold of me and begins to raise me to a new level of living, I discover my aim in life becoming different. Suddenly I find myself saying good-bye to some things I know in order to say hello to a lot of things I don't know.

Hoover Roopert, Methodist pastor and author, once told of a *Washington Post* reporter's account of the maiden voyage of a cruise ship on the Potomac. The ship was built to carry passengers from Mount Vernon to Washington, D.C. All kinds of Washington dignitaries gathered for the trip, including Congressmen and Senators and Cabinet officials. The ship steamed out into the river on a very hot, humid, muggy day.

One Congressman sitting by the rail took off his shoes and socks. Suddenly someone running down the deck knocked one of his socks over the rail and into the water. "Now," said the reporter, "this Congressman did a very impressive thing." Without hesitation he picked up the other sock and dropped it over the rail too. The reporter found that impressive because he knew exactly what he would have done. He would have taken the remaining sock home and kept it in his drawer for a year until he could figure out what to do with it. And I would have probably done the same. Yet, how much more sensible it is to just say good-bye to the useless sock, as the Congressman did.

That is exactly what I hear these words in the New Testament asking me to do when they say, "Aspire to the realm above, where Christ is." Doing that means saying good-bye to some things I have gotten used to in order to say hello to a lot of things I have not yet experienced. It means having the courage to let go of that old sock. I can't assume that a new life in Christ will help me to determine how to use that old sock. I simply have to say good-bye to it. And as I do my aim in life changes. For instance, I don't have to aim at money the way I once did. Not because I think money is evil. I don't. And it isn't. I simply no longer have to aim at it as an end in itself. Christ has raised my eyes to see that if I do, it will swallow me up. As my aim changes, money becomes not an end in itself. I now see it as a means to an end. I see it as a means of accomplishing God's purposes. In money, God gives me the power to do his will in this world, in my home, in my community, through my church.

Furthermore, as my aim in life changes, I find I can say good-bye to trying to please everyone. There was once a time when I tried to do that. What a deadly and subtle temptation for anyone to fall into. Yet I find that as I allow Christ to raise me to a new level of living I am free from feeling threatened because everybody's heart doesn't skip a beat when I walk into the room. By saying good-bye to trying to please everyone I discover a new freedom to become myself—the self God calls me to become. Now I can aim at that without deliberately hurting anyone.

For me, the miracle of Easter is the new accent it puts on life. Every time I read and reflect on the story of

Jesus raised from the dead, I find myself moving out into
life with a brisker step—shoulders back and head up—for
I know that even on the freeways and side streets of this
world "my life lies hidden with Christ in God."

He Is Not Here

John Killinger

And when the sabbath was past, Mary Magdalene, and Mary the mother of James, and Salome, bought spices, so that they might go and anoint him. And very early on the first day of the week they went to the tomb when the sun had risen. And they were saying to one another, "Who will roll away the stone for us from the door of the tomb?" And looking up, they saw that the stone was rolled back—it was very large. And entering the tomb, they saw a young man sitting on the right side, dressed in a white robe; and they were amazed. And he said to them, "Do not be amazed; you seek Jesus of Nazareth, who was crucified. He has risen, he is not here; see the place where they laid him. But go, tell his disciples and Peter that he is going before you to Galilee; there you will see him, as he told you." And they went out and fled from the tomb; for trembling and astonishment had come upon them; and they said nothing to anyone, for they were afraid.

(Mark 16:1–8, RSV)

IMPLICATIONS OF THE RESURRECTION

Scripture: Romans 6:1-13; Colossians 3:1-10
I Corinthinas 15:12-23

CHR-

Introduction

The facts which surround the historical reality of the Resurrection of Christ are as well
known as these of the Christmas story...the mean
ing of those facts..like the meaning of those
surrounding the birth of Christ...is not so evi-
dent..if we are to judge by their manifestation
in the lives of believers...FOR A FULL, COMPLETE
UNDERSTANDING OF THOSE FACTS ALONG WITH THEIR
REAL SPIRITUAL IMPLICATIONS IS LIFE'S MOST TRANS-
FORMING EXPERIENCE WHEREVER AND WHENEVER A BE-
LIEVER RESPONDS WITH TOTAL LIFE COMMITTMENT.

It is the function of worship to impress upon
the mind and heart of the believer the glory of
God..to see the possibility of that glory surrounding even the most ordinary situation of our
lives...to be aware of the implications of great
beliefs we hold and to inspire and encourage the
worshipper to live..and die...as though the meani
of truth was one and inseparable from his existence. IN VIEW OF THE GENERAL SHALLOWNESS OF OUR
LIVES AS CHRISTIANS THE IMPLICATIONS OF THE
RESURRECTION OF CHRIST OUGHT TO BE DISTURBING TO
MOST OF US...TO SAY THE LEAST. If you go away
disturbed about certain aspects of your life as
a Christian this message will have achieved its
purpose...if you decide to make certain complete
and radical changes in your attitudes..your habit
your motivations...your daily deeds..it will be
the doing of the Holy Spirit through the WORD OF
GOD...

As we view the story of the Resurrection of
Christ and Paul's doctrinal interpretation of it
we are confronted by at least two tremendous
truthes....

I have a confession to make to you. For years, on Easter Day, a little voice somewhere inside of me has said, "This is all make-believe. It isn't real. You are pretending to something you don't really believe." The same voice has often raised itself at funerals. "It's nice to pretend that there is life after death, but you can't really believe it."

Some people may be shocked at this admission, but I know that I am not alone. Some of you have felt the same way. You feel a little guilty at admitting it, as I do, but the truth is that you have always been a little skeptical about the Resurrection and life after death. It seems like a great big fairy tale at the heart of the Christian faith, complete with lots of sunshine and the smell of Easter lilies. And you suspect, the rest of the time, that the whole Christian religion has slipped a peg or two since the days of the early church, because they—those wonderful early Christians—believed it and it energized them in all they did. We are failures for God today because we're such half-hearted believers. We can't even believe in the Resurrection.

Well, I have a word for you. Most of the early Christians had trouble believing it too. I discovered this only recently. I was restudying the Gospel of Mark, which most critics agree is the earliest of all the Gospels in our New Testament, and I kept puzzling over the ending.

There seems no doubt, you know, that the original version of Mark—at least of the part we have—ended at verse 8 of chapter 16. All those other verses—the ones that are printed in all the modern translations in small print—were added by somebody at another date. They aren't in

the style or language of Mark or whoever the original
author was.

"Why would Mark end his Gospel here?" I
kept asking. He talks about the Resurrection—there is this
fellow in white, obviously an angel, at the tomb, saying,
"He is going ahead of you to Galilee"—but he doesn't show
us the resurrected Jesus at all. It's as if he gave a resurrection
party and Jesus didn't come! "How strange!" I thought.
What could Mark have intended?

Then I remembered two stories from back in
earlier parts of the Gospel. One was in the sixth chapter of
Mark, about Jesus walking on the water one dark and stormy
night. The disciples were out in a boat—fishing, I suppose—
and a terrible storm came up. They weren't making any
headway in the boat, when suddenly they looked out and
there came Jesus walking across the churning waves. They
thought he was a ghost, the Scripture says, and they were
terrified. But he said, "Fear not, it is I," and got in the boat
with them, and the winds and waves subsided.

It is a puzzling story until you realize that it is
a Resurrection story. It isn't in the place in Jesus' biography
we would expect, but that's what it is. The "ghost" thing is
a giveaway. And when Jesus says, "It is I," the Greek is
really *ego eimi*, which means "I am." You have to wonder
if Mark was thinking about that time when Moses met God
at the burning bush and God told him to go lead the Israelites
out of Egypt and he said, "Who shall I tell them sent me?"
And God answered, "Tell them I Am sent you." I Am—
Jesus in the storm, looking like a ghost and saying, "Don't
be afraid, I Am." But then, Mark wasn't writing ordinary
biography—he was onto something else.

The second story I remembered was in the
ninth chapter of Mark. You'll know what it is if I say it is
the transfiguration narrative. Jesus took the disciples
closest to him—Peter and James and John—and went up
into a mountain to pray. That is important—why they were

there. And late in the night, just as in the story of the stormy
sea, which was also late at night, the disciples saw something
that made their eyes pop out. They were very sleepy, says
Mark—could barely stay awake—when suddenly something
happened that made them forget all about sleep: They saw
Jesus transformed into a wholly new self, with a glowing
face and a bright, shining robe. And he was talking with
Moses and Elijah, two men who were dead—had been dead
for centuries!

Now this was another Resurrection story. Again
out of place, but a Resurrection story. Afterwards, after
the vision, everything went back to normal. Jesus looked
the way he had looked before, and the men were gone who
had been talking with him.

What was Mark intending by this? No
resurrected Jesus at the end of his Gospel—only the
instructions to go into Galilee and watch for him there—
and two Resurrection appearances pushed back into the
Gospel all out of sequence with the story of Jesus' ministry.

Now, as I puzzled about this, something else
about Mark kept gnawing at me. There is another theme in
his Gospel that seemed related to this. The theme of
watching and *understanding*. All through the Gospel, Mark
represented the disciples as seeing everything with their
eyes but nothing with their hearts and understanding. They
kept missing the point. They saw Jesus feed the multitudes
in the wilderness and then they worried because they had
no bread to eat. They heard him talk about suffering and
then they asked for first place in the Kingdom and said he
could never be crucified. They listened as he said they would
all deny him, and they swore it would not happen. And
here at the end, in the Scripture we read, the women saw
the angel and ran off in fear and didn't tell a soul—not our
usual picture of Easter morning at all. They never seemed
to catch on, they never understood.

And Jesus kept talking in the Gospel about

watching. Watching to see. Watching to understand. It
becomes very specific near the last. At the end of chapter 13,
which is a chapter about "last things," Jesus tells a little
parable about the master who goes away, leaving his servants
in charge of his house. He tells them to watch for his return.
One of them is even stationed at the door and cautioned not
to leave it, so he can see the master the minute he is coming
and warn the others. "Blessed is the one whom the master
finds watching," says Jesus.

Then there is the passage in chapter 14 about
Gethsemane. Immediately following the Last Supper, Jesus
takes the disciples—all but Judas—and goes to the garden.
He leaves most of them in one place and goes farther with
the inner circle of three—the ones who were on the mountain
with him—and tells them to watch and pray with him.
Then he goes a bit farther alone and kneels to pray. Presently
he comes back and finds the disciples sleeping. He wakes
them up and tells them to watch and pray. He goes back,
prays some more, and again returns to find them sleeping.
A third time, the same thing. What is going on? It isn't a
story about Jesus' great devotion. We know that. It is a story
about the disciples. They didn't watch and pray. Their Lord
came and found them sleeping. They didn't live up to the
parable. They didn't see and understand. They wouldn't
believe the Resurrection. They would run away and be
silent.

You see how it all begins to come together,
and how much like us they were? Resurrection was hard
for them too. They had their experiences of the resurrected
Jesus, but these weren't on Easter! They were back there
in the midst of life—once when they were out fishing at night
and once when they were praying in the mountains. But
not on Easter morning.

That is the way it is with us. We sing and
talk about the Resurrection on Easter, and then feel a little
guilty that that voice inside says it all may not be real. But

our real experiences of the Resurrection are like theirs—
they occur in the midst of life, when we are fishing or
praying, when we are making the beds or walking along a
country road or reading a book or burying a friend or walking
through the supermarket. And the word to us, like the word
to the disciples, is to watch and pray. That's the secret—to
watch and pray.

If we haven't seen any manifestations of the
risen Christ lately, it is because we haven't watched and
prayed. We haven't "practiced the Presence," as Brother
Lawrence called it. Some of us have been so lax about this
that we don't *ever* really believe in Resurrection and the
afterlife any more. Not at Easter or any other time. We don't
ever see the resurrected Jesus. We don't ever hear a
heavenly voice or feel a divine confirmation. Our whole
"Christian" life is a sham and a pose, and the only reason
we don't give it up is that we don't know what else to do.
You see, Mark understood something you and I must
understand—that watching and praying are the foundation
of the whole Christian experience. There is no other way
to have the Christian experience, no other way to see and
feel and understand it. If we are not willing to spend fifteen
minutes or more a day in absolute quietness of spirit, listening
and waiting on God, so that that centering time converts the
rest of our day into a day spent with Christ, then we cannot
enter into the vision of Kingdom life the Gospel is
talking about.

I once joined a learned society. It was an
important international group. I was invited to become a
member, and I was flattered and excited and sent in my
annual dues. They had overseas meetings and all, and I
thought, "How romantic, how wonderful. I am so glad to
be a member." And I remember when the time came to
attend my first meeting. It was to be held in Ireland, in
County Cork, a perfect setting. I bought my ticket and
was prepared to go. But the time came and I had other things

to do, and I worried that I would miss my family and I
didn't go. And I have never been to a meeting since. I
receive the annual papers of the society, and sometimes I look
at them, but for the life of me I can't get excited about them
because I wasn't there when they were given. I am a member
but I am not really into it.

Has your Christian experience been that way?
You are a member but not really into it? You don't really
understand it? It's impossible to understand it without
watching and praying, without the time in meditation and
reflection when we open ourselves to the Lord's presence
and learn how to see him in the common places where our
days and nights are spent. That's where Jesus meets us. Not
on Easter. Not at the empty tomb. But out there in the
common places. Out where we work and shop and bank
and eat and fight and make love.

"Tell the disciples—and Peter—" he said, "I go
ahead of them into Galilee." Galilee was the place of their
ministry. All of it but the last week had been in Galilee and
the north countries. That was where they would find Jesus—
back in the familiar places where they labored. And it is
where we shall find him as well, my friends, not among the
lilies and choirs and padded pews—if we learn how to watch
and understand.

Christ the Lord is risen today,
Sons of men and angels say.
Raise your joys and triumphs high,
Sing, ye heavens, and earth reply,

       Alleluia!

Lives again our glorious King;
Where, O death, is now thy sting?
Once he died our souls to save,
Where thy victory, O grave?

       Alleluia!

Love's redeeming work is done,
Fought the fight, the battle won.
Death in vain forbids him rise;
Christ has opened paradise.

       Alleluia!

Soar we now where Christ has led,
Following our exalted Head;
Made like him, like him we rise,
Ours the cross, the grave, the skies.

       Alleluia!

Charles Wesley, 1739

Introducing the Writers

The writers whose spiritual insights illuminate the pages of *The Miracle of Easter* are both gifted communicators and valued friends and colleagues. In one way or another each has contributed liberally to my own pilgrimage of faith, and for this I will ever be in their debt.

Each writer very perceptively views the Easter event through a slightly different set of lenses. But as these scenes are brought together through prayerful and receptive reading, we begin to see a *Whole* forming which gives us a clearer glimpse of the magnitude of the Miracle of Easter.

JAMES ARMSTRONG, Bishop of the United Methodist Church, Dakotas area. Prior to his election to the episcopacy in 1968 he served as senior minister of Broadway Church, Indianapolis. Bishop Armstrong has served his denomination on numerous boards and agencies and is the author of a dozen books.

MAURICE M. BENITEZ, Rector of the Church of St. John the Divine, Houston, Texas. Before taking his theological work at the School of Theology, University of the South, Dr. Benitez served in the United States Air Force for six years. He is a graduate of the United States Military Academy, West Point.

ERNEST T. CAMPBELL is involved in an at-large ministry working out of New York City, which includes writing, guest preaching, lecturing, conducting retreats, and leading workshops for ministers in Homiletics. He formerly served as senior minister of Riverside Church, New York. Dr. Campbell is the author of three books and has been visiting lecturer at Princeton Theological Seminary, Pittsburgh Theological Seminary, and Fuller Theological Seminary.

JOHN KILLINGER, a professor at Vanderbilt Divinity School in Nashville, Tennessee, and the author of some twenty books. He travels extensively, speaking to church and college groups, conducting seminars on prayer and worship at summer assemblies and for the U.S. Air Force in the Orient.

JAMES I. McCORD, President of Princeton Theological Seminary; also President of the Association of Theological Schools in the United States and Canada. Dr. McCord has been actively involved as a churchman on a worldwide basis since 1948. He is chairman of the Editorial Council of *Theology Today*, editor of *Supplementa Calviniana* (Calvin's hitherto unpublished sermons), editor (with T. H. L. Parker) of *Service in Christ*, editor (with Paul Empie) of *Marburg Revisited*, and editor (with Edward J. Jurji) of *The Phenomenon of Convergence and the Course of Prejudice.*

DAVID L. McKENNA, President of Seattle Pacific University, Seattle, Washington. He has served in leadership capacities in several educational associations, including the Washington State Council on Higher Education, the Association of American Colleges, and the Christian College Consortium. He has written extensively for publication, his most recent books being *The Jesus Model* and *Contemporary Moral Issues for Evangelical Christians.*

JÜRGEN MOLTMANN, Professor of Systematic Theology, University of Tübingen, Germany. Among Professor Moltmann's extensive writings are the following books: *The Crucified God, The Theology of Hope, The Experiment*

Hope, and *Man: Christian Anthropology in the Conflicts of the Present.*

JOHN P. NEWPORT, Vice President for Academic Affairs and Provost, Southwestern Baptist Theological Seminary, Fort Worth, Texas. Dr. Newport has written four books, including *Christianity and Contemporary Art Forms,* and has lectured extensively on Christianity and the Arts at universities and seminaries in the United States and in Mexico.

ROBERT A. RAINES, Director of the Kirkridge Retreat and Study Center in northeastern Pennsylvania. Dr. Raines is the author of ten books, including *New Life in the Church, To Kiss the Joy, Living the Questions, Success Is a Moving Target,* and *Going Home.*

FULTON J. SHEEN, one of the foremost and best-known Christian spokesmen and writers in the United States. An outstanding orator, colorful radio and television personality, preacher, and former bishop of Rochester, New York, he was Titular Archbishop of Newport (England) at the time of his death in December 1979. His sixty books include *Guide to Contentment, Life Is Worth Living, Peace of Soul,* and *The Wit and Wisdom of Fulton J. Sheen.*

ARTHUR FAY SUELTZ, minister of Lakewood First Presbyterian Church, Long Beach, California. He is the author of four books, including *If I Should Die Before I Live.*

FLOYD W. THATCHER, Vice President–Editorial Director, Word Books, Publisher. Writing credits include four earlier books, among them *The Splendor of Easter* and *The Gift of Easter.* He is co-author with Charlie Shedd of the Christian Writer's Seminar program with cassette tapes and workbook.

ALAN WALKER, Director of World Evangelism for the World
   Methodist Council. Dr. Walker is probably Australia's
   best-known churchman, having led the work of Central
   Methodist Mission for twenty years. When he is not travel-
   ing on preaching missions he preaches to Australia's largest
   Sunday evening congregation in Sydney's unique church-
   in-a-theatre. Dr. Walker is the author of over twenty books.

HAROLD C. WARLICK, JR., Director of Ministerial Studies and
   member of the Department of Applied Theology, Harvard
   University Divinity School. Prior to his present position
   Dr. Warlick served as minister of Southern Baptist churches
   in South Carolina and Texas. He is the author of three
   books, the latest of which is *Conquering Loneliness.*